Mail Order Bride

A play

James Robson

Samuel French — London
New York - Toronto - Hollywood

MAIL ORDER BRIDE

First performed at the West Yorkshire Playhouse, Leeds,
on 28th November, 1994, with the following cast:

Martin Hindshaw	Timothy West
Ivy Hindshaw	Rosalind Knight
Maria Bongay	Swee-Lin
Joe Garbut	Mark Addy
June Garbut	Morag Siller
Additional voices	Lyn Belshaw, Caroline Bird
	Robert Bird, Purita Richele
	Michael Rudko, Karen Tan

Directed by Jude Kelly
Designed by Paul Andrews
Lighting by Mark Pritchard

CHARACTERS

Maria Bongay, 35. An attractive Filipino woman; intelligent, shrewd, tenacious, humorous and direct. She retains optimism, hope and common sense despite many bad experiences with men. An able secretary who lost her job due to sexual harassment, she became a bar girl in Manila under the name of "Coco". She speaks English well, peppering it with (sometimes obscene) Americanisms and enlivening it with the peculiarly Filipino habit of using clichéd phrases in everyday speech. It would be fair to say that she has not a complete sense of right and wrong but a strong sense of natural justice. A fiercely determined volatile streak runs beneath her cheerful compliant exterior. Although experienced and wary about men she has a genuine desire to be loved and valued and cared for in an equal relationship. Her singing voice is a discordant disappointment. **NB**: For the two short Filipino passages in the text, some research may be required — in the original production the actress playing Maria spoke a mixture of Singaporean and Filipino.

Martin Hindshaw, 50. A farmer on the Yorkshire Wolds. A craggy bachelor who lives with his sister and has become lonely, obsessive, and addicted to work — he is emotionally and sexually immature in this isolation. A passably handsome, rugged man thickening with age and letting himself go. Touchy, shy and old-fashioned, he is dumb about his inner state and his longings have recently found expression by listening to classical music and watching mild porno videos. He has a dark taciturnity enlivened now and then by shafts of dry, droll humour. A big man who expects little from life, running a modern "agri-business" with competence and pride. It is more than probable that he has never known a woman intimately or carnally. A kind but rather sad and limited man who has grown fond of making money. He has an almost symbiotic relationship with his sister Ivy.

Ivy Hindshaw, 55. Martin's sister. Small, powerful, stately spinster, who has "done" for both Martin and herself domestically since the death of their parents. Her bright-eyed countrywoman's face belies her nature, which has become sarcastic, inquisitive, jealous and hypochondriacal. Heavily influenced by her dead father, she is religious, judgmental, prudish and bitter, with a prissy, caressing tongue which can turn whiplash in an instant when required. Manipulative, sometimes terrifying, sometimes pathetic — she is an undeveloped personality clinging to old certainties. Loveless and static, she is capable of smiling sweetly with hate in her heart. She has remained the little obedient "Daddy's girl" who bossed Martin around as a child and has ordered his days until the present. She was a village schoolteacher until she left because of ill-health (and irascible resistance to change). She has a wicked sense of humour and — her saving grace — a strong sense of right and wrong. Her undeclared love for Martin borders on the obsessive and incestuous — it is the binding, strangling attachment of ivy to a dying tree. She once taught Joe Garbut.

Joe Garbut, 30. Martin's farm labourer. A local cricketer, footballer, darts player and one time hard-man of the Wolds who might have done better for himself and lives on past parochial glories. He lives in a council house in the nearby village. He is married to a fat, loyal scrubber whom he often wishes he'd never set eyes on but needs, even loves, in a battered, pained, limited way. Beginning to feel his age and lack of satisfaction, he drinks heavily and can be a dangerous drunk. A dry, flip joker most of the time with a line in frank rural banter — beneath the "couldn't give a damn" surface he is the archetypal trapped working-class male sublimating his immense frustration into booze, sport, sudden violence, hard work and rock music — the latter being almost a drug to him. Has an extensive record collection (the antithesis of Martin's) which he hires out for local events with himself as laconic DJ. He carries a huge ghetto-blaster everywhere on the farm as a bulwark against silence and thought. He has the usual vague fantasies of leaving the North and the domesticity he despises (but needs) and of "making it" somewhere else. Not a talented person or a stayer, he is promiscuous, parochial, shallowly romantic and incapable of facing up to himself and life. A dreamer and drifter, he is handsome in a (slightly dissolute) way. He carries the baffled anger of one who can imagine how his life might be but is not capable of achieving such change.

June Garbut, 26. Joe's wife. She is letting herself go in all directions. Once pretty, she has now run to fat, the victim of too many cigarettes, too much coffee and gin, and a general lack of purpose. She loves Joe in a sullen, disgruntled, occasionally close-to-screaming-violence way, though he bewilders and scares her much of the time. Soft, lumpen, sentimental and basically thick and dependent, she seems unable to properly understand her situation, let alone do something about it. She's a child-woman and a "townie" at heart who loathes the lonely village with its closed community and lack of amenities. Although badly mismatched with Joe and misused by him, she clings to her narrow dominion, knowing that Joe somehow needs her and always goes back to her, thus far at least. She and Joe had a child (Tracey) who was taken into care two years ago. She cleans house for the Hindshaws one day per week.

ACT I

SCENE 1

The large kitchen of Starfits Farm, on the high Wolds of North Yorkshire. Friday, May 1994. Late afternoon

The farm is a typical grain-producing establishment with limestone buildings, a shelter belt of ancient sycamores, phallic grain silos and driers under skies almost as wide as those in Texas. It is devoid of animals and surrounded by vast fields without hedges. It has an isolated, bleakly beautiful atmosphere

The kitchen is a spacious but sombre room kept obsessively clean by Ivy (and her mother before her). All the surfaces are wiped clean and clutter-free, an old oak dresser is polished, everything is in its place. There is an Aga stove extreme L, and near to the back door to the farmyard, C, a short passage with work boots on the floor and clothes on pegs. To the L of the door there is a sink, beneath a half-lace curtained window suggesting a view across the yard to the field gates; sycamores and sheds. An archway, R, leads to the passage to the front rooms of the house and DR there is an open staircase to a landing and the bedrooms, etc., with a newel post. In the alcove under the stairs is an "office" area, with a farm computer and monitor on top of a kneehole desk, a swivel chair and an anglepoise lamp. There is a CD player on the shelf above the desk and a number of record stackers containing Verdi, Vaughan Williams and Mozart CDs, all purchased from mail order companies. There is a dresser with blue and white china on display on racks, and, R, a long table with chairs — one of them, at the head, is a high-backed Windsor chair, "Father's Chair", and respected as such. There is a small colour TV with a VCR and rack of videos, a sofa near the Aga, food cupboards near the window, a calendar of Yorkshire views and a pile of farming weeklies and mail order catalogues. On the dresser are family photos in good quality frames, including a striking one of Mr and Mrs Hindshaw on their wedding day, circa 1944. They are a severe and uprighteous couple

The late afternoon sunlight glints on the window and the gilding frame of the back door, which is ajar. "O Soave Funciulla" from La Bohème *comes from the CD player. Martin stands by the sink gazing out across yard. He is ill-at-ease in smart trousers and shirt. Ivy is seated at the table poring idly over the outspread* Yorkshire Post, *sipping tea. She regards her brother as he sighs and turns back into the room*

Ivy Father would be pleased ...

Martin stares

You taking to proper music. (*She stares along the table to the Windsor chair*) I can see him now listening to concerts on that old battery set ... Saturday nights. Terrible reception.

Martin sighs

The applause seemed to go on for hours at the end, like a sea.

Martin walks to the door, opens it a shade more and gazes across the sunny yard, then walks back to the table. He sighs again

Don't sigh, Martin. No good wishing you hadn't done it now.
Martin I'm not. (*He glances at his watch*) Friday afternoon traffic must be murder.
Ivy Sometimes I know what you're going to say before you open your mouth ...

Martin sighs

Just as well because you don't consult, do you. Take this new obsession — (*glancing at the CD player*) suddenly that thing arrived, and the funny little records, and the books about great composers — I could have told you about Mozart and Verdi .... Things build up with you so slowly don't they? If you'd just said about this whole thing (*taking in the whole room at a glance*) we might have talked it out.
Martin Talked it out of me you mean.

She looks at him. He keeps his eyes on the door

Always done it, mebbe that's why I don't consult.

Ivy takes the teacup and saucer to the sink, rinses them, puts them on the draining board, and goes to the TV

Ivy I should know the signs by now I suppose.
Martin What signs?
Ivy Period of immense broodiness, silences, monosyllabic exchanges for

days, then — out of a blue sky — surprise .... (*She runs her finger along a rack of videos*) Sudden interest in videos, that was a surprise — but I understood, I took it on board.

Martin Everybody has videos now ——

Ivy I don't mind your videos — not even the ones Joe Garbut brings you on a weekend, the ones you play when I've gone to bed ...

Martin sighs, chastened but indifferent

I try not to condemn anyone, just because I think it's all so sleazy (*she guffaws falsely*) — heavens knows I daren't go in a video shop let alone take one of those to the counter! "Lovers' Guide" — what would Father have said if he found one of those in the house?

Martin Things people do is up to them ——

Ivy Lying in bed listening, sorting out the day in my mind — I thought this is a strange film, not much dialogue .... That's why I came down. I wasn't prying.

Martin shrugs, sighs, walks to the window and stares out

Is the sound important? I think it'd put me off — not that I'd watch.

Martin Oh no, no ...

Ivy Fairly limited activity isn't it ... Why anyone needs a guide is beyond me ... (*She stops and stares at his broad back*) You're so like Father from the back, our Martin. He would have understood the music, been glad about that ... (*Cocking an ear to the duet*) Balm to the soul isn't it ... ?

Martin sighs

Don't sigh, Martin, it's tiresome. You've always done it, quite without thought or reason — (*she sighs*) since school days in fact.

Martin starts, and stifles another sigh. Ivy smiles at him

In the desk behind mine, sighing ... I loved the autumn, nights closing in — reading in here, doing my homework (*looking around, imagining*) by the hissing tilly lamp. Father in his chair, tired, nodding to the radio ... Mother always busy, baking or darning ...

Martin Why are you saying this?

Ivy (*with an edge*) Why the love duets, the arias — after years of indiscriminate listening? Why the mucky videos ——?

She stops, they stare at each other, tense

I shouldn't have said that, sorry.

The CD ends

Martin What does it matter?
Ivy You're my brother, I'm interested in everything you do — I shouldn't
have expected you to stay the same — I didn't — but why this — why now?

Martin shakes his head

Perhaps if you'd expressed these — desires to me, I might have helped,
shared ... Martin? (*She picks up a video from the "Filipino Friendship
Agency" and reads the title out loud*) Why?

Martin sighs

Stop it! (*Pause*) I realize there are limits to our relationship, Martin, but I
have tried ... to talk.
Martin You never just talk to me, there's always something at the back of
it ...
Ivy Nonsense ——
Martin Always a drawback, a reason not to do — a hidden agenda. (*He
stares at the severe couple in the photo frame*) You're like him. I never did
anything to his total satisfaction. Seedtime, haytime, harvest and never a
word of praise ... I've cut turnips hour after hour, crying with the cold and
tiredness and he never once said: "Well done, good lad, Martin" — just that
dour presence, judging me ...

Ivy crouches to the VCR with the video in hand

What are you doing?
Ivy How do you start this thing? I want to see it now.
Martin I wanted you to see it when I said she might be coming ——
Ivy (*interrupting*) Was coming Martin, was packing her case in Indonesia
or Bongo Bongo Land or wherever ——
Martin You know exactly where ——
Ivy Only since I came across her airmail letter and you had to tell me — a
fortnight ago! I mean were you just going to let her arrive on the doorstep?

*Martin presses the "play" button on the VCR. Ivy stares pugnaciously at the
screen, arms folded. (The screen is out of view)*

Might as well see her before she does — reduce the culture shock.

Martin picks up the control and fast-forwards the introduction and several jabbering female Filipinos

Very similar, aren't they? Though I suppose they say that about us ... I thought you liked blondes. You had this thing about Kim Novak I remember — Mother found those photos under your mattress ... *(She stops as Maria appears on the screen)* Is she the one?

Martin nods, gazing at the screen image

I can see the attraction of course.

Maria giggles, charmingly girlish

Oh she's shy poor thing ... Can she speak English? I hope she isn't short — or squat — some of them tend to be I believe ...
Maria's voice My name is Maria Bongay, I am twenty-six years old ——
Ivy Really ...
Maria's voice — and looking for someone to love and respec' me ...

Martin pauses the tape. (The image quivers)

Martin She works in Manila Hospital.
Ivy She is dishy, Martin, I have to admit — not absolutely sure about twenty-six but still ... *(she giggles)* perhaps I can check her teeth at some point!

Martin flicks the VCR off

What is she Martin?
Martin *(sighs)* How many more times ... She's Filipino, a decent Catholic woman ——
Ivy Details ... What do you really know about her?
Martin That's what she's coming for ——

Ivy puts the video back in the carton

— so that we can ... *(He shrugs)*
Ivy *(reading from the carton)* "Explore your loving potential" ... Well, I begin to understand the other videos now — explorers do need guides after all ...

Martin stares straight ahead as she tightens the screw, regarding him, circling slowly

No need to be embarrassed, Martin, God knows I'd be happy to see you exploring anything after all these years — but this woman? After a correspondence? (*Kinder, smiling up at him*) I mean ... I know you must have felt lonely at times — I have, I'm not insensitive to the demands of the flesh — I am aware what men are like about the physical side of life ...

She stops as Martin glares at her

Martin Lonely. (*Pause. He gathers the full meaning of the word to himself*) Loneliness ... (*He thinks about it, turning on the rack of memory before her*) I've had nowt else ——

Ivy (*a reflex*) Not "nowt", Martin ——

Martin Nowt — nowt else but — I've lived on it, eaten it for breakfast, dinner and supper and gone to bed with it — driven up and down those bloody fields with it all day for days on end ... (*He stares at the sofa*) Worked till dark, till daft times — so I could come in here and drop on that sofa and get out of it (*he snaps his fingers*) like that ... I've dreaded coming through that door into this — bugger all ... (*He regains a measure of composure. Softly*) Don't tell me about loneliness, I'm made of it.

Ivy (*hit*) Who's been up there (*glancing at the stairs*) listening for the latch? You never said ... (*She seems about to touch him but instead goes to the dresser and stares at the photo of the wedding couple*) Have you considered how they would feel about this?

Martin (*dully*) They're in churchyard, Ivy.

Ivy Must be spinning under that grass ...

Martin sighs hopelessly

Stop sighing, stop it for God's sake! If you knew how stupid it sounds ... (*She stops and holds her lower stomach, hunched slightly by the table, fingers splayed on the front of her skirt*) Sorry but you know I'm not well, I've got a splitting headache all the time and my ovaries are playing me up again ... Can't lift so much as a pillow without them pulling at me ...

Martin stares, impotent, he's heard it so many times. There is the sound of a vehicle pulling up in the yard and he goes quickly to the window and gazes out. Ivy follows as far as the Windsor chair and stops, holding on to the back. We hear the snatch of a song on the radio, Bruce Springsteen's "Born in the USA", until it is cut off by the sound of car doors slamming shut

Joe Garbut enters with a Rattan case in his hand, face closed. Maria, dressed as demurely as a nun except for sunglasses, follows and stands in the sunlight, framed in the doorway

Joe turns to look back at her. They all stare at this exotic vision

Joe Bloody M1 you wouldn't believe it — talk about a rat run ...

Ivy watches like a woman of stone as Maria comes into the room and takes off her sunglasses, blinking, staring at Martin

Martin Maria ...
Maria (*shocked*) Martin ... ?
Martin Welcome to Starfits Farm ...

He's obviously stunned by her presence, deeply stirred and delighted but also embarrassed and afraid. He flaps his hands towards Ivy, who is imbibing her first impression like poison

Meet my sister, Ivy ...

Maria smiles, lighting up the sombre room. She goes towards Ivy with a hand outstretched

Maria Ivy ... I am so glad to meet you! How do you do!

Ivy smiles falsely as she takes the hand

Ivy How do you do.

She drops the hand and the two women regard each other

Quite a journey, you must be tired out.
Maria (*sensing a chill*) Not too bad thank you.

There is a moment's hiatus, broken as Joe puts the case down and sings a phrase of "Maria"

Maria (*to Martin*) You got crazy man working for you — he sings to radio all way from airport! I tell him to shut up after while.
Joe In no uncertain manner ... (*He laughs and sings another phrase from the song*)

Martin picks up the case

Martin Well thanks, Joe lad.
Joe Don't mention it.

Martin takes the case to the foot of stairs and looks up the flight, then across to Maria

Martin Your room's on the landing, third door on the left — bathroom's at the end if you want to freshen up ... after your journey ...

Maria smiles. Joe backs towards the door, grinning

Joe I'll be off then, so long, Miss Hindshaw.
Ivy Stay and have some tea if you like ...
Joe (*shaking his head*) Friday — (*to them all*) wife's shopping day, has to "get out into civilization", she says ... (*He goes out, grinning*) Scarborough ...
Maria Thank you, Garbut!

Joe laughs as he exits, the sunlight hitting him

In the ensuing silence Joe is heard getting into his pick-up and gunning off down the road to the thumping strains of Meat Loaf's "Bat Out of Hell". Ivy heads for the stairs

Ivy If you'll excuse me ...
Martin Don't go, Ivy ...
Ivy (*suddenly pathetic*) I need to go and lie down, Martin. (*She pauses by the case*) I'd take your case up but my ovaries ... Can't lift a log for the fire some days ...

Ivy exits

Maria Ovary?
Martin (*nodding wearily*) Had 'em all her life ——

Maria giggles

—— I mean, trouble with them — and migraine, and arthritis, cystitis, thrush, continual backache. If she leaves her body to medicine they'll have a field day ... (*He stares at Maria, the words petering out*) Your video ... doesn't do you justice, Maria Bongay.
Maria You are older man than your photo, Martin Hin'shaw.

Martin is hit, staring

Why send all young photo?
Martin All I had ...
Maria You disappoint me, Martin, I think you are good respeccable man —
English gentleman farmer — but you play trick on me.
Martin I'm sorry ...
Maria You are much older man (*studying him*) grey as volcanic ash — I
don't think I want old grey man ...

Martin bears her scrutiny, wordless and full of pain

Don't they have camera on Yorkshire Woles yet? Nikon? (*Snapping an
imaginary camera at him*) Canon Sureshot? If you send recent photo I
never come here OK!
Martin OK ——
Maria Not OK! Before I even get here you lying to me — you must
understan' my feeling?

Martin nods, dumb as a bullied child in the playground

(*Softening her tone*) I come all this thousands of mile in good faith, give
up helluva job in hospital, leave my whole family ——
Martin I know I was wrong —
Maria Man on plane with pig-breath coming on strong to me all way — say
well if you get off on wrong foot with your English gentleman farmer give
me a ring ... He give me his card but I leave it on plane — I think we getting
off on wrong foot right?

Martin nods. Pause

You old as hills. Tomorrow I go back home please.

*Martin stares. Maria sighs, tired. She walks to the newel post and picks up
her case*

You mention bathroom? I dying for hot bath.
Martin At the end of the landing.
Maria (*staring at him, sad but determined*) It best like this, I come and go
like Spirit of Air and it hurt less all round — OK? You think you had dream.
(*She starts up the stairs*)
Martin Just like that ...
Maria Yes! If your sister not here I wouldn't stay in house one night with
dishonourable old man.

Martin I paid your fare ...

Maria So? You think you bought me or something ...

Martin No ... I've been waiting that's all, sort of thinking I had a future ... (*Staring up at her*) One night ...

Maria (*still angry and wary, but kinder*) One night with you is what I praying for too, Martin Hin'shaw. You write young letters, I read them over and over — they give me hope to carry on — strength to leave home — they full of longing for love and promise of happiness — who you get to write them — Joe Garbut?

Martin shakes his head in vehement denial. He puts a hand on the newel post and stares after her ascending figure

Martin You never lied ... About your age for instance?

She stops and turns calmly

Maria OK I thirty-five years old — they told me at the Agency to say twenty-six — I didn't like to but they say Western man want only young Filipino woman, younger the better eh ... (*Flashing with sudden anger*) Teenager is good. Child sometimes, sometime baby it not surprise me, like Manaboas Monkey ... (*She checks her tongue*) I thirty-five, how old you, grandad?

Martin I knew you wouldn't come if I sent true photos ——

Maria So what you plan to do — wear mask all time with young man's face on?

Martin I thought if I could just get you here ——

Maria (*sadly sarcastic*) I so charmed by your personality I decide to stay? (*She shivers*) Is cold 'ere, is this summer on Yorkshire Woles?

Martin Spring ...

Maria I die in winter here. (*She turns away*) Don't worry, Martin Hin'shaw, I pay your money back somehow.

Martin (*half shouting*) I don't care about that ——

She suddenly turns her face back to face him, wide-eyed, staring down

I don't give a bugger about the money ... Do you have to go?

Maria Yes! You think I desperate or something? (*Exasperated, she slips into jabbering Filipino: "Can't you see how you've fucked me about. My friends give me all night send-off and now I crawl back like beggar ... You make me lose face! They think I am fucking fantasy merchant! They think I liar!"*)

Martin What?

Maria I go first thing in morning!

Martin (*shaking head*) Saturday's bad for travel, Maria — I'd have to check flights ——

Maria I go somehow! Taxi! Stagecoach! I get back to airport somehow and I go that is all — I go home!

She scrambles off with her case

There is the sound of a slamming from along the landing. Martin looks up the polished length of the table to the empty Windsor chair

Black-out

SCENE 2

Saturday morning

The sun is shining in through the window and the back door, which is ajar. Birdsong. Martin is hunched at the table with a mug of tea as Ivy takes his breakfast plate to the sink and returns to stand at his elbow. The Rattan case stands in the sunlit passage

Ivy She's cutting it a bit fine.

Martin sighs; a frown flickers across Ivy's face

Don't sigh, Martin. (*She stares at his profile, gauging his mood*) Anyway it's for the best, you've been sensible. You'd always have wondered ——

Martin I found nothing out ...

Ivy First impressions are very telling I find. She seems straightforward but doesn't give much away, she's deeper than you think ——

Martin She hasn't gone yet, Ivy.

Ivy No, (*glancing to the door*) but I do think when she has ——

Martin stands up abruptly, almost upsetting his chair. He stares as:

Maria enters from the yard, smiling as she sees him. She has a bunch of common grasses in her hand

Maria Morning again!

Martin nods

Ivy Morning.

Maria Oh what a beautiful morning ... (*Holding up the grasses*) Aren't they beautiful?

Ivy Rather common grasses — I didn't know you'd gone on a nature ramble.

Maria (*dashed*) I think I take them with me — put in book for souvenir.

Ivy You ought to have something to eat before you go, some toast at least?

Maria (*shaking her head*) This some ranch you got here Martin — middle of nowhere with nothing in sight all around ...

Ivy I love the plain views, you can see the sea on a clear day — a sparkling horizon. I hate clutter.

Maria I can see clearly now the rain has gone — I can see all obsticle' in my way ...

Ivy stares blankly. Maria giggles

  Is like ranch on Oklahoma, Martin, or the High Chapparal!

Martin Just a Yorkshire farm, Maria ...

Maria But no animal! I always think of English farm with fat animals in fields.

Martin (*patiently*) It's arable land you see ——

Maria Horrible?

Martin (*amused*) It's for growing crops — heavy land but fertile.

Ivy Been well-worked and cared for that's why ... (*she glances at the photo*) for generations ... They always put something back, never just robbed the land.

Maria drops the grasses on the table and picks up the photo

Maria Parents?

Ivy (*with a twitch*) On their wedding day ...

Maria Look like they going to be shot. (*She giggles*) Hope I look happier when I ——

Ivy takes the photo from Maria and replaces it on the dresser gently but firmly. Maria looks hurt

Martin We've no call for animals now.

Maria (*recovering*) You got plenty big machine in sheds.

Martin These are broad acres ... Three hundred acres down to wheat, one hundred acres to barley, fifty to Golden Wonder spuds — and the rest is oilseed rape and "set aside" ...

Ivy (*disgusted*) Set aside ——
Martin Common agricultural policy ... They're paying us to take land out of production these days ... Leave it fallow.
Ivy (*snorting*) Father would have loathed the idea — leaving whole fields to go sour, weed infested ...
Maria So you master of all you survey Martin.
Martin (*proud*) S'pose I am.

Ivy gives him a cold glance

(*Catching this*) Ivy has a share of course.
Maria You are English gentlewoman farmer, Ivy?

Ivy stares coldly

Martin Ivy was schoolteacher in the village till they closed it down a few years back ...
Ivy Twenty-five years of service ended in a day ...
Maria (*sadly*) Oh that shame, Ivy. Teacher is good — in Philippines you get much love and respec' ...
Ivy (*bitterly*) How all things end isn't it — in a day, with little warning ... (*She pulls herself together*) Martin you must allow time to get Maria's ticket — they're slow as wood in that ticket office.

Martin heads heavily for the door

Martin I'll bring Volvo round ...

He stops as we hear the pick-up stopping in the yard. There is the sound of doors opening and a burst of music, "Satisfaction" by the Rolling Stones. Martin looks at his watch

Twenty minutes late, that's not bad for him ...

Joe enters with a ghetto blaster blasting. June trots in behind

(*Flapping a hand at him*) Turn that bloody row off!

Joe does so, grinning

You should have been here at eight o'clock.
Joe Why what happened? (*He saunters to the table and drops a couple of*

bills in front of Ivy. In a gormless Yorkshire voice) Postie Postie don't be slow, be like Elvis, go man go ... *(Grinning at her)* Morning, Miss Hindshaw. Morning, Maria ...

Maria Morning, Garbut.

Joe Eh? You can call me Joe ... *(he tugs his forelock at Martin)* if that's alreet, maister?

Martin ignores him, and stands at the door looking skyward. Joe notices Maria looking at June

Ah sorry, this is my wife — June.

Maria Hallo, June.

June Hallo.

June looks shattered, reduced by Maria's presence. Joe can't take his eyes off her

Maria You like to have photo, Joe?

Joe Wouldn't mind a centrefold — *(grins)* any more like you at home?

Maria Oh yes. *(Fondly)* Maria number two, Marcia, Epiphania, Susanna, Paul, Pippi, Joe, Anya — and last but not least — Donna — youngest of family.

Joe That's not a family it's a tribe.

Maria *(sadly)* Yes, only chief die — my father drink like fish — one night he walk into Jeepney *(she smacks her fist into her palm)* he real real gone ...

They stare at her as she regains control. Martin plods back into the room proper

Martin *(to Joe)* Get that spraying finished Friday night?

Joe *(his eyes still on Maria)* Drive belt kept slipping — lost a bit of time — I'll finish it this morning.

Martin Crack on then, that barley's mucky as hell — watch drift — stop if wind gets up. You hear?

Joe *(dragging his eyes away from Maria)* Yeah, yeah — you'll be fetching us some Sportak?

Martin When I get back from station.

Joe Station?

Ivy Maria's leaving.

Pause. Joe and June absorb this. Since no more information is forthcoming he shrugs and offers Maria his hand

Joe Merry wind to you then, Maria.
Maria Merry wind?
Martin He means goodbye.
Joe Sorry to see you go. (*Grinning and taking her hand*) Last exciting thing
that happened up here was when grain silo got struck by lightning and
spilled its guts over yard ... nineteen eighty-five ...
Maria Merry wind, Joe Garbut.

*Joe stares a moment longer then goes out, toting his ghetto blaster. Martin
follows*

Ivy looks at June

Ivy Start re-arranging the dirt any time you like June ... Front rooms?

June heads for the passage arch

Maria Goodbye, June.
June (*going*) Bye ...

June exits

*Maria and Ivy regard each other. A large tractor barks into life in the near
distance. Maria extends her hand to Ivy*

Maria Might as well part like friends, Ivy ...
Ivy (*taking her fingertips briefly*) I don't make friends overnight I'm afraid.
Maria No, you got nothing for me but smile on stick. (*She imitates a wooden
fixed smile*) So what did I do wrong?
Ivy If you don't know I hardly think it's worth trying to explain ——
Maria I come in good faith, on invitation from your brother ——
Ivy I've looked after Martin's interests since he could walk — since they died
(*she glances at the photo*) I've done everything for him for years — and
what does he do? He sends for another woman, a total stranger — by mail
order ...
Maria Mail order ... Me?
Ivy He likes sending for things — music, seeds, clothes — it's become an
addiction. He spends hours looking at catalogues, making out orders ... it
makes him feel important I think — everything on approval, sale or return
— but I have to send them back ...
Maria You think he send for me like this — like stupid doll?

Ivy He doesn't know his own mind, he's a bairn in some ways — he was
terrified when it hit him you were actually on your way. (*She gives a false
guffaw of mirth*) He'll be so relieved when that train pulls out, believe me ...

Maria Hey this is my life you talking about ——

Ivy You don't know the first thing about him — he has fantasies — he
couldn't cope with you — the strain'd kill him, he's a bairn, a child ——

Maria He write good letters, man's letters ... He say he long for woman of
his own, to be in house when he come in from fields ...

Ivy is hit, splaying her fingers across her belly

He say he lonely as hell and want partner on farm ——

Ivy I'm his partner ... (*Struggling for control*) I've been here for him all his
life, how could he say such things — as if he had no-one ... He must have
been fuddled — sitting down here brooding, drinking Scotch — he
probably wrote those letters half ... He can't have been thinking straight!

Maria You only his sister when all said and done ——

Ivy Only?

There is the sound of a car pulling up in yard

I'll be here for my brother long after he's forgotten all about you, Miss
Bongay. (*She holds on to the back of Father's chair*) You had no right
coming here, what kind of woman would come after a few letters? — you
can't have much self-respect, or shame!

Maria Why should I be ashame'?

Ivy (*with towering condescension*) It's not the way we do things here —
Englishmen don't buy Englishwomen from catalogues, it just isn't done!

Maria You telling me Englishwoman don't take all she can get in marriage,
don't take house, don't take nice clothes, car ——

Ivy It's not the same!

Maria stares, quizzing her: "Oh no?"

Why am I arguing with you — your life has nothing to do with mine and
Martin's ...

June enters through the archway with polish and duster and stands staring

Maria All I want is to be free like Western woman — maybe have honest
relationship with respeccable Englishman ...

Ivy A little wog woman like you ... (*She stops, shocked at her own words*)
Sorry. I shouldn't have said that ——

Maria Is better out than in ——
Ivy No, it was uncalled for ——
Maria Is no wonder Martin want woman from my country if all English
women are cold boss bitches like you ...

Ivy controls herself with an effort

Martin enters and stares at the three women

Martin Ready then ...

He senses the atmosphere

What's going on? June?

June shrugs. Ivy heads for the stairs, holding herself

Ivy?

Ivy starts to ascend the stairs. Martin stares at Maria and picks up her case

Maria What you think of Maria Bongay so far Martin Hin'shaw? You
approve of mail order woman or she not what you desire?

Martin stares. Ivy stops on the stairs

She say you little boy looking for plaything when you ask me to come on
finance visa (*sic*) — that true Martin?
Martin No.
Maria You rat-arse when you write to me Martin?
Martin No.
Maria You really want to explore loving potential with me, Martin?
Martin Yes ... (*He notices Ivy's look*) Yes ...
Ivy (*softly*) Don't do this to me ...
Maria Finance visa OK for three months, yes Martin?

He nods

Then I think I give it three months, make or break.

*She takes her case from Martin and heads for the stairs. As she reaches the
newel post, Ivy comes down unsteadily and holds on to it, ashen. She revolves,*

eyeing Maria as she passes. Maria starts to ascend. Martin crosses the room and stares up

Martin You're going to stay ...
Maria All things considered, giving it fair crack of whip an' all that ... (*Smiling*) I think I suck it and see — yes Martin!

She exits

Martin's expression exults, until he sees the Medusa-like face of Ivy. But he is defiant

Black-out

SCENE 3

The following Monday. Lunchtime

Joe and June are lounging at the table with coffee. She is smoking, he is eating sandwiches from a tin. Joe's ghetto blaster is on low: "Here Comes the Night" by Them. Joe is preoccupied, June is prattling ...

June I dunno how they get away with it ... Fifty pence difference in price ... Bloody supermarkets — they're a law unto themselves they are ...
Joe Where is she? (*He sits in an armchair*)
June Her ovaries came on ... (*She puts the back of her hand to her brow, imitating Ivy*)

Joe grunts, amused

I nearly said: I could do with a lie down myself. Two pounds a bloody hour!

Joe stops chewing and sniffs a sandwich

Joe What is this. Whiskas? Pedigree Chum? Only the best. (*He tosses the sandwich crust into the tin*)

June It's potted beef.

They listen to the song

Used to like this record didn't you.

Joe Still do.
June It's whatsisname isn't it ... You know?
Joe Them.
June Them? I don't remember them ——
Joe Irish group, good, under-rated.

She stares at his profile, his indifference

June We don't do much for each other any more do we? Even when we go
out we don't have a laugh or anything.
Joe (*flat*) Gimme a break ...
June Them ... You sure?
Joe (*switching the ghetto blaster off*) Them ... Leader singer Van Morrison
— Van the Man — all right?
June (*hit by his tone*) It's only a record, I was only asking — trying to make
conversation.

Joe gets up, walks to the sink and stares out of the window

I've seen married couples out together you know — sitting, talking, having
a good time.
Joe (*turning*) Say something then.

June stares

Say something I haven't heard ten thousand fucking times before — that
doesn't make me groan (*with his fist on his chest*) in here, doesn't make me
feel so tired and pissed off I want to crawl into a corner and die ... Say
something?

*He sits at the table and starts to roll a cigarette. Hit even worse, June gets up
and scrabbles her lighter and cigarettes into her handbag*

June I'm going, I'm not sitting here like this ...

Joe shrugs, rolling a cigarette. June stares down at him across the table

You'll do that once too often, that shrug — you'll do that one day and I will
go ...

She leans on the table and glares into his downcast, impassive face

Say something to me. I don't make things happen, I just wait — and nothing happens. I hate my life, I hate that bloody council house and that (*glaring upwards*) poison dwarf up there. I should never have let you bring me here — last place God made. Most men live where their wives have always lived but not you ... (*Hit*) If I could get Tracey out of that place I'd ——

Joe What — go back to Mummy?

June I'm not a bad mother! If you'd helped me, done more — I'd have coped!

Joe You locked her in and went on bloody walkabout not me ——

June I was going mental. (*She stops, pained*) Mummy, she says ... why can't I come home, Mummy?

They both stop, pained. Pause; they stare. Joe sticks his roll-up in his mouth and stands up

Joe (*rough but not unkind*) Go home ... keys are in pickup.

He closes his lunch tin and pushes it towards her. June stares dumbly, then something gives in her

She picks up the tin and handbag and goes wearily out through the back door

Joe stands for a moment in thought. The pickup starts-up outside

Ivy comes downstairs looking tired, wan

Ivy What's all the noise?

Joe shrugs, listening to the vehicle going away. Ivy walks to the end of the table

Is that June going? I haven't paid her.

Joe Always another day. (*He picks up his ghetto blaster and heads for the door*)

Ivy Can you see how ruthless she is, Joe ...

Joe (*stopping*) Nah, she's just thick ——

Ivy Her, I mean — Miss Bongay — they are ruthless you know, they're not like us ... My Uncle Ray was in the Chindits fighting the Japanese — he knew what they were like.

Joe (*grinning*) The Chindits? That a sixties group?

Ivy Inhuman, he said — slit your throat for your bootlaces ... They're all the same.

Joe (*slightly embarrassed*) That's not what you used to tell us at school, miss
— tolerance you said — all people are basically OK ...

Ivy What are they saying in the village?

Joe Nowt that I've heard.

Ivy They will, we'll be the laughing stock.

Joe swings towards the door

How does she make you feel?

*Joe looks at her from the sunlit passage. There is the sound of a Volvo
entering the yard and stopping. Joe shrugs*

When you saw her at the airport how did she strike you ... ?

Joe This isn't fair, miss ... (*He scratches his head*) I didn't feel anything
much. She treated me like a bloody chauffeur — sat in the back and went
to sleep after a bit ... I kept looking at her in the mirror ...

There is the sound of car doors slamming in the yard. Joe looks out

They're back.

Ivy How do you feel now, Joe?

Joe (*staring out*) Like I knew this'd happen some day ...

Ivy Yes, anything else?

Joe (*bleakly, matter of fact*) Like my whole life's been a sodding waste of
time ...

He smiles as:

*Maria enters, smiling, refreshed by her outing. She loses her bounce when
she sees Ivy standing by the table*

Maria Hi, Joe ...

Martin follows her, carrying shopping bags

Martin Late lunch, Joe lad?

Joe Just going ...

Martin puts the bags on the table. Ivy smiles her smile on a stick

Ivy Shopping ... Had a nice time?

Martin Took Maria for a bar snack, thought she might like to see a traditional Yorkshire pub.

Ivy (*that smile; to Maria*) And did she?

Maria I like very much, good pub grub but beer like monkey pee. (*She giggles*)

Ivy I wouldn't know. (*She flutters a hand across her brow and heads for the passage, pained*) I've got a terrible head today, excuse me.

Martin Ivy ... We've been talking ——

Ivy stops

—— about the three of us. Can't we try to get along —— just until things are —— sorted out like?

Ivy Sorted out like ... What does that phrase mean exactly, Martin?

Martin Until we see —— (*flapping a hand towards Maria*) whether we've got a future ... That sort of thing ...

Ivy What about my future, Martin? Where do I fit into your new world order —— unpaid skivvy? Mad sister locked in the west wing —— or do you have residential homes in mind?

Martin Don't be silly ...

Ivy heads off into the passage to the front rooms

Ivy ...

He follows her off

There is the sound of a door along the passage. Joe watches Maria take a new small cassette recorder and a blank tape from the shopping bag

Joe Saw you out walking early on ...

Maria (*inserting the tape*) I like to get out of house. You were on big tractor yeh?

Joe nods

This Starfits looks like farm but smell like hospital everywhere ...

Joe Grammoxone, Sencorex, Round-up, Sportak —— (*he grins at her*) Agent Orange ...

She just stares back

It's spraying this time of year.

Maria No animals?
Joe (*grinning*) Only me and Martin.
Maria You work here long?
Joe Too bloody long.
Maria You don't like being farm hand?
Joe (*shrugging*) It's a job.
Maria You don't like Starfit Farm?
Joe You've seen it. (*He shrugs*) There's nothing out there since Martin
 ripped the hedges out ... Twenty-five acres one way, twenty-five acres
 back ... Nowt but seagulls and sky and dust — sweat running into your
 eyes — jogging up towards the house and going away again like a friggin'
 android ... (*He hoists the ghetto blaster from the table*) If I didn't have my
 music ... (*He pulls a lunatic face, flapping his tongue*) Funny farm ... Knaw'
 mean?

Maria giggles, setting up a tiny microphone for the tape recorder

Maria So what you do when you not on funny farm?
Joe Football, cricket — got stack of records I play for discos, parties,
 weddings ...
Maria You are DJ? You famous in England?
Joe In Bridlington.

Maria giggles, Joe laughs. We hear the door in the passage

  They love me in Brid.
Maria You big star in Brid yeh!

  Martin appears in the archway

Joe (*drily*) Colossal ...
Martin You still here.
Joe Drive belt?
Martin It's in the car ... (*Exasperated*) Didn't I say?

Joe shakes his head

  Come on then!

  Joe follows Martin out into the yard

Maria sits in the Windsor chair at the head of the table, composes herself and speaks into the microphone

Maria Hallo, Mama, Nana, and everyone ... Well I have been nearly two weeks already at Starfit Farm which is like big house on prairie ... House belonging to Martin Hin'shaw is very old and solid as rock with old furniture inside and — (*looking around*) big stove called Aga which you would love, Mama ... Martin is a bit older than I expec' but I think I maybe get to like him and you can't judge a book by looking at the cover ... I think he is a kind and generous man but shy ...

She glances to the sunlit doorway as we hear the Volvo boot slam shut and the men's voices grumble, off

Martin has man called Joe Garbut working for him who make me laugh ... (*She glances at the dark archway*) And ugly old sister with rotten ovary who does not like me much ... Feeling is mutual and I deal with her if she want trouble ... I am a bit afraid of her because she like witch — but don't worry ... There is Landrover here, Volvo car and many farm machines but no animals yet. Water is always scalding hot and I have had bath every day with oil and soap from Body Shop ... Already I am making myself at home. (*She wipes a sudden tear away*)

Martin enters quietly and stands listening

I am thinking about you all, very much — first thing in morning and last thing at night — I pray for you all by name — especially my darling little Donna ... (*She looks at Martin and stops the tape*) I sorry I get Ivy mad again, Martin.
Martin She'll come round.
Maria Her bark worse than her bite maybe?
Martin (*moving to her side*) No her bite's bloody awful as well ...

He smiles and she smiles back

Tape recorder all right?
Maria Oh yes, Martin, wonderful surprise for family — much better than letters for them.

She stands up and pulls his face down by his jacket lapels and kisses his stolid cheek

Thank you, Martin. (*She sits again*)

Martin is dazed by this simple expression of gratitude

(*Gazing at the china on the dresser racks*) You got lovely china plates, Martin, cup and saucer, jugs all blue and white ... My Nana never have one good plate in her life — you eat off this plate, Martin?
Martin Sundays sometimes, special occasions — Mother used them a lot more ... She loved her willow pattern ...

They both see Ivy in the archway, rigid, holding herself and glaring at Maria

Didn't she, Ivy ... ?
Ivy A word Martin please.

Martin looks to Maria

Maria picks up the tape recorder and heads for the stairs, quickly but with dignity

(*Going to the sink and picking up a cloth, then moving back to the Windsor chair*) I won't have that person in my kitchen, Martin, do you hear? I won't have her messing about in here ... (*She starts to rub the seat of the Windsor furiously*) Sitting here, doing things I know nothing about, moving things so I don't know where they are — touching things, Martin ...

Maria hears all this before she exits upstairs

I won't have it ——
Martin All right, all right ——
Ivy You'd better make sure she understands ...

Martin watches her furiously rubbing the seat of the chair, speechless

Have your way in this charade of a relationship if you must, Martin. Take her pubbing and shopping and showing her the sights — make an utter fool of yourself as much as you like — but not in here, not in my home!
Martin She only wants to help, Ivy ...

Ivy slumps a little, calming herself and staring at him

Ivy (*wondering*) I can't seem to get through to you. When I took a new batch
of children into school I could always tell how bright they were by looking
into their eyes — as long as I could see that spark of intelligence there I
knew I could teach them ... (*Staring into Martin's eyes*) The times I've held
a smelly little farm lad and looked into baffled bovine emptiness, Martin ...
Martin What are you on about?
Ivy Boys, men ... (*She sighs*) We study you all our lives and you never see
us half the time. Did you even try to imagine how much this would hurt me?

Martin heads for the door, fearful, baffled

Martin I've work to do ——
Ivy Ay go and play with your tractors ——
Martin (*wrenching the door open*) Be in a fine mess if I didn't!
Ivy I do not want this woman in my life in any capacity, Martin! Are you
receiving me?

Martin goes out, hunched, sulky, angry

I don't want her!

The Lights darken on Ivy standing by Father's chair

Black-out

SCENE 4

Night, a week later

*The kitchen is dimly lit and empty. The chairs are on top of the table. Car
doors slam in the yard and giggling ensues*

*Maria enters through the back door. She is wearing a red dress (brought from
the Philippines) and carries a handbag. She is followed by Joe and June.
They are all dressed for fun and rather loosened by drink. Maria puts her
handbag on the table*

*Joe switches the ghetto blaster (still on the table) on: "Twisting The Night
Away" by Sam Cooke. Maria puts her handbag on the table and warms
herself by the Aga, giggling. Joe watches her*

Martin enters through the back door and regards them all

Martin I don't know what's so funny ... D'you, June?

June shrugs. She and Martin regard the giggling Joe and Maria

Laughing at nothing all way up the road ...
Maria It so funny at disco, Martin!
Martin Blummin' loud I know that ...
Maria Yorkshire people dance so funny! (*She demonstrates a stately, spastic, agricultural-type churning twist, in front of the Aga*) Like this!

Joe laughs and joins in, piss-takingly awful

Martin That's me is it?
Maria (*doing it worse*) Oh no, Martin ...
Joe (*ditto*) No, Martin ...
Martin I haven't danced in years, I'm a farmer not Fred Astaire. (*He turns the blaster off and looks to the stairs*) Ivy'll be in bed.
Joe Ay don't wake the undead.
Maria (*smiling at him*) I did enjoy it, Martin, I love dancing out my skin now and then.
Martin I noticed.
Joe What about the DJ?
Maria Oh he not bad. (*She giggles*) "Welcome to Young Farmers' Disco — let's kick off with: 'I Got Brand New Combine Harvester'" — what is that song about?
Joe Got to give the punters what they want — played your request didn't I?
Maria (*twisting again, sinuously this time*) If you looking for love baby I'm — tougher than the rest!
Joe (*partnering her, close*) Put on your red dress baby 'cos we're going out tonight ...

Maria sees June and Martin, isolated, and stops. She goes towards them with Joe

Maria I see you and June jiving — very good.
Joe (*staring at June*) We've had some practice. Met at a village dance didn't we? (*He sings to June*) "Well my heart went boom when I crossed that room" — she couldn't believe her luck ...
June (*to Maria*) He could hardly stand never mind dance, he had sick on his shoes and kept missing my hand ——
Joe (*hit*) Never! We danced like a dream ...
June Glad you think so. (*She checks her watch*) Look at the time, it's nearly Sat'day morning.

Joe Nobody ever refused me a dance anyway.
June Daren't probably, if you weren't drunk you were rolling about the floor
   fighting. (*She turns and heads for the door*) Come on, I'm worn out.

Joe turns to Maria

Joe I like a woman who drinks pints — next time we jive.
Maria OK, Mr Famous DJ.
Joe All I need is a break ...
June Been saying that since nineteen seventy-nine — "Gimme a break".
   Night, Maria, Martin!

She goes out

*Joe holds Maria around the waist and grins, a reprise: they sing the first three
lines of the chorus of "Do You Wanna Dance", alternately. They laugh and
gyrate together sexily for another moment*

Joe kisses her and goes

*Martin bolts the back door. There is the sound of the pickup leaving the yard.
Martin watches Maria swaying and humming by the Aga: "Do You Wanna
Dance". Martin takes the kitchen chairs down, replacing them around the
table*

Martin Like a nightcap, Maria? There's Ovaltine, Horlicks, cocoa?
Maria Yes? (*She turns, startled, hand to mouth*) Why you call me that ...
Martin What?
Maria Some people in Philippines call me Coco. (*She thinks*) Did I mention
   that?

Martin shakes his head, puzzled

   I didn't think I did ...
Martin Your friends at the hospital?
Maria No, other friends ...
Martin Why Coco?
Maria (*shrugging*) I forget, is not important — you mean hot chocolate
   drink!
Martin Coco — I like it ——
Maria I love hot chocolate! (*She sings in her croaky voice a couple of lines
   from "It Started With a Kiss"*)

Martin I think I'll call you Coco ——
Maria No, Martin. (*Staring at him*) Maria is my name, please ...

He stares, and goes on staring — hit by the simple, startling fact of her presence in the familiar sombre room. He stares so long she giggles nervously

Martin, what is it?
Martin Dammit I never know what to say.
Maria (*touching her bosom*) Is easy Martin, say what in here. (*Pause*) Say it, Martin.
Martin I can't believe you're here.
Maria I can't believe I am — I feel like tourist — you show me so many places — Railway Museum, York Minister ...
Martin Minster ...

She smiles

Sorry about that lot at the Wolds Inn, staring all the time.
Maria I don't even notice, I used to that ... (*Checking herself*) I mean, so what — they can look but they better not touch eh?
Martin You shone out in that room — dancing — you knocked 'em dead ...

He moves closer as she stands against the warm rail of the Aga. She senses his mood

And me ... I know it's early days Maria ——
Maria You can't hurry love Martin, you just got to wait ...
Martin I know that ——
Maria (*smiling*) Love don't come easy ——
Martin That's it, though, that's the word — I just need to know it's still on the cards, like ...
Maria (*teasing*) I think you ask all women this, Martin — you take to Young Farmer disco and fill with pints of big John Smith and bring back here for cocoa? (*She smiles up at the huge, serious, bear-like man and touches his lapels, softening*) I don't think you had much fun in your life, Martin Hin'shaw ...
Martin I love the way you say my name.

She smiles up at him sadly then turns her back, holding on to the Aga rail

Maria We both know I don't come all this way for holiday — but I got to be sure — we both got to be sure.

Martin stands close behind her, staring at the nape of her neck

My Nana is old Igorot woman who smoke pipe on porch all day —
tribeswoman ... In her wildest dreams she never think of owning anything
like this ...
Martin An Aga?
Maria (*turning; giggling*) Farm, Martin! Big house with land all around,
sheds, machinery — safe place for family, place to enjoy wonderful life.
Ranch like Southfork ... (*Wondering herself*) Security, money in bank,
respec' of neighbours ... I got to believe you really want me to have all this
Martin — for ever and a day.
Martin Yes, all that ...

She goes to him on tiptoe and puts a finger on his lips

Maria You got to be sure you want Maria one hundred per cen' ... All she
got in world is in case in bedroom and what you see in front of you. You
must understand, life is harsh in my country, we sure of nothing, not even
next meal sometimes — and we desperate because we want better lives for
our children and family and ourselves ...

Martin nods

We see our lives going to waste and it kills us inside — we all want good
life ... We do crazy things sometimes to get it.
Martin I'd say you could have a wonderful life. Anything must be possible
for a woman like you ...

Maria smiles sadly and takes his right hand

Maria I never met shy man before ... Man who listen to me so carefully ...
All time we been going to places — you pay everything and say it
"Gentleman's privilege" — I never hear that before. You open all doors,
put chair under me to sit in pub and restaurant — once we bump together
in doorway and it like I burn you with my hip ... Is taboo in Yorkshire to
hold hands in street maybe? Hug somebody?

Martin stares down at her, amused, touched; she lets go of his hand

In Philippines is good to hug, to touch — everywhere except private parts
and top of head — pat on head is bad insult ... People get killed for that. Oh
Martin ...

She hugs Martin, he stays immobile. She tries to kiss him on tiptoe but can't reach. She stands on his shoes and thus succeeds, kissing his chin and cheeks, giggling

Loosen up, Martin? Is like hugging tree!
Martin You're on my feet.
Maria (*giggling*) Walk me, Martin!

He walks towards the back door and she rides on his shoes, light, lovely, laughing softly like a girl. Martin chuckles, embarrassed yet intoxicated

Ivy comes dazedly into the archway from the front room, clutching a novel, blinking in the light

My father used to do this when we little — all of us in turn until he tired out — you like giving me walk, Martin?
Martin (*laughing*) Makes a change! Could be a bit awkward across fields though ——!

He stops as he sees Ivy. Maria sees her and dismounts. She goes slowly, downcast, to the Aga. Martin stands, sheepish but defiant under her gaze

Ivy Have you locked up, Martin?

Martin nods. Maria picks up her handbag from the table and heads for the stairs

Maria Thank you for night out, Martin. Good-night.

She exits

Martin watches her go. Ivy regards him

Ivy If you could see yourself ... (*She shakes her head*) Where have you been till this time? Not carrying on like that in public I hope.
Martin Wolds Inn ...
Ivy That gossip shop, doing what?
Martin Dance — Young Farmers ...
Ivy Young Farmers? How come they let you in?

Martin walks to the Windsor chair and slumps into it, gripping its arms

Making a show of yourself with — that ... (*She glances at the empty stairs*)
If you can't think of yourself consider me — and the family name.

Martin It's nineteen ninety-four, Ivy, I'm almost fifty ——

Ivy Then for God's sake act your age ——

Martin I'm tired of acting my age ... Sometimes I think I was born middle-aged ... "Old Martin", that's what they called him (*gripping the arms of the chair*) and soon as he died I got it: "Old Martin" — steady, boring old Martin. (*With bitter pain*) Salt of the bloody earth.

Ivy So why throw that respect away? Can't you see what she's after — I've a share in this business ——

He gives her a hard look. She stops

Martin My farm you mean ...

Ivy Our farm, Martin, our inheritance ——

Martin This place I've sweated my guts out on since I were lad, no not even a lad — a bairn?

Ivy You got the son's share ——

Martin Who else? Who put his life into it — picked it up and made it viable?

Ivy He taught you well, Martin ——

Martin He knocked it into me ... I used to milk five cows before school every morning, remember? Sat in class with cow hairs down my sleeve — the other lads used to laugh at me when I feel asleep at my desk. (*Mooing*) Ma-a-a-artin! Wake up Ma-a-a-artin ....

Ivy Some things never change, Joe reckons you're talk of village over that woman. A laughing stock.

Martin I don't give a shite.

Ivy Don't say things like that! How dare you sit in that chair and ... (*She falters*) I don't know what's come over you, she's changing your very nature. (*Closer, staring at him, sniffing*) You reek of alcohol .. she's turning your head ——

Martin (*realizing it*) Turning my life inside out ... I was waiting to die, now I'm living for the first time.

Ivy Stupid ... (*She is hit*) Infatuated at your age — why are men such fools? A bit of cleavage and a few come-to-bed looks and all your brains fly out of the door ... Mother was right — you're slaves to your animal natures ...

Martin It's more than that, Ivy ——

Ivy I don't want to hear about it! Don't bring love into it, don't talk to me about *love* ...

Martin stops in the face of such cold fury

I thought you were my rock and sure foundation. (*She can't find the word she wants, struggling beside him*) It's so unexpected of you — unseemly — unfair!

Martin I'm a man, Ivy ... I know you always did your best to ignore it, as they (*glancing at the photo*) did ...

Ivy Now you're talking gibberish ——

Martin They kept me like a monk here and you like a nun, they drilled work and religion into us and kept us away from life ——

Ivy Don't you denigrate them ——

Martin You knew it, Ivy, only you didn't seem to mind ... (*Clapping his palms on the chair arms*) He ruled us from this bloody chair, you there (*looking to an empty chair*) me there (*another*) Mother serving on like a dumb beast ... He used to read the paper to us remember? All the agonies of the world outside — war, famine, cruelties — hedging us in with horrors, making Starfits seem like the only refuge, the only place to be ...

Ivy He loved us, wanted to keep us safe ——

Martin He wanted to keep us, for work — to look after him in his old age — and stay children all our days ... He had our lives mapped out — (*staring at her*) stick to your studies, Ivy, never mind the lads hanging around ...

Ivy It's now we're talking about, you and her!

Martin When did we get out to dances like other kids our age? Used to hear the band sometimes — the "beat" as they called it — thumping across the Wolds ... Started to see faces we knew in wedding photos in the *Gazette*, and heard bells ringing some Sat'day mornings if wind was right ... (*He glances to back the door*) Wedding bells, Ivy, children, family life — happiness ... (*Pause*) Love.

Ivy (*hit*) Tell me you're not going to marry this woman, Martin ... Please?

Martin (*dragging his gaze from the door*) When she came through that door a month ago I felt such pain — such confusion, I thought I might be having a stroke ...

Ivy Lord knows I've nothing against you getting wed — but to this woman ... ?

Martin I not only saw what might be possible in a life — I saw what I'd missed all these years ... You can't begrudge me this chance, Ivy.

Ivy You know nothing about her, Martin! You can't see what she is because you're besotted — I know she's mercenary and as cunning as the Devil — women know other women!

Martin stands, angry and weary of this

Martin It's none of your business.

Ivy stares, shocked. Martin walks to the CD player and presses it on. He stands with his back to Ivy, longing for the first strains of Verdi. She heads for the stairs, hunched and hurt. He senses this and softens, looking her way

Ivy, I've wanted this that long, longed for it ...

She stops on the stairs, looking up

Can't you be glad for me?

Pause. Ivy shakes her head a fraction, then exits

Martin turns as the music begins and seems to plunge into it, bowing his head down over the CD player. He is bull-like, hurt. The Lights fade on him

Black-out

SCENE 5

Mid-afternoon. Ten days later

Sunshine. Poultry sounds from yard. In the kitchen there are signs of mail order acquisition: a new cafetière, slow cooker and toaster. Maria sits at the table speaking into her tape recorder

Maria I really beginning to think I have found good man who will love and respec' me — Martin my English gentleman farmer who is so kind to me — everything I like he send for by mail: toaster, electric kettle — I have lots of things he send for already. (*She looks slightly doubtful at the array of gadgets in front of her*) Is pity I can only use some of them when Poison Dwarf not in ... I know I can be good woman here but I am not sure how I feel all time ... (*She looks towards the sunny doorway*) English weather is shifty, sun just comes and goes as if not sure of its own mind — and there is always wind on these Yorkshire Woles — big trees called sycamores always rustling around outside ...

A hen cackles triumphantly outside

I got a dozen hen called Rhode Island Red who are laying already — Martin bring them from market last week and Poison Dwarf look daggers ... Anything I want I only have to mention ... Oh, I hope Nana like tobacco I send and English pipe? Golden Virginia is very big in Yorkshire ... (*Suddenly sad*) Please tell Zeny and everyone I am happy and expecting proposal any time — I love you all so much, especially my little Donna — maybe you will send photo of her sometime?

She breaks up a bit, hand over her face. She ejects the tape and inserts another. Filipino voices fill room, the distant family speaking all at once

Nan's voice (*old lady*) Hallo Maria my pretty one — send me more tobacco eh? I love you ——
Maria 2's voice Hi Maria! How is life in England? You met her Majesty the Queen yet?
Paul's voice Let me talk to Maria! Hey Maria, send me something eh? Send me some T-shirt, Maria ——
Maria 2's voice Mamma say when you going to send some money Maria? Things are not so good here financially ——
Mamma's voice (*her mother, weary*) Maria .... (*Shouting at the others*) Shutup and let me speak! I not feeling too good again ... I miss you ... I taught Donna some words to say, my daughter ——
Donna's voice (*a four year old*) Mummy ... Are you there? I love you, Mummy. I miss you, Mummy ... why have you gone away?

Joe enters unnoticed, a filthy paper mask under chin, the silent ghetto blaster in his hand. He is grubby, dusty and hot. He stares at Maria's intent, bowed figure

Joe Martin about?
Maria (*startled*) Joe! You frighten me. (*She switches the tape recorder off*)
Joe Thought you had some people in here — your people ...
Maria (*longingly*) Some day maybe ...

Joe walks around her, frankly studying her in full circle. She giggles

What you doing, crazy man?
Joe You're perfect... You haven't got a bad side, every way I look at you—you're perfect.
Maria Nobody perfect, Joe, I got bad side. You just haven't seen it yet.
Joe (*shaking his head*) Where is he?
Maria Gone into town.
Joe Without you ...
Maria She go, so I don't go.
Joe Getting on any better? (*He puts the ghetto blaster on the table and starts to roll a cigarette*)
Maria She act like I'm invisible most of the time — or she got smile on stick — she leaves pots after meal and I wash up and dry ...

Pause. Joe regards her

I don't know what happen if Martin ——
Joe (*finishing the sentence for her*) Pops the question?

Maria shrugs and stares around the room

No justice is there. You come all this way — Martin's like a dog wi' two
tails about you — but there's Poison Ivy ...
Maria You expect justice? Nobody in Philippines expect anything but hard
work, broken dreams — kick in teeth from life.
Joe Peasants round here don't even dream.
Maria They not peasants, Joe. I know peasants.
Joe Hicks from the sticks then, narrow-minded, thick as shit nobodies ——
Maria Not like you eh?

Stung, Joe lights up his cigarette

Joe I can do better than this, I come from round here but I can see other places
(*he touches his head*) in here. Other lives, one hundred per cent satisfying
lives, not this (*looking round as if the walls were closing in*) narrow-gutted
existence.
Maria Is hard work to make dream come true, Joe, you have to be strong,
tougher than the rest — (*looking around too*) then it not always like you
think.

Joe stares at her, drawing on his cigarette

Joe No money, that's been my let-down ... No bloody brass — that's why
I'm still here on misery bloody farm ...
Maria Is same problem all over world — if Martin hadn't sent money I not
be here ...
Joe Oh he's loaded, bloody farmers are all the same ...
Maria Maybe we shouldn't talk like this, Joe ...
Joe When I saw you coming across that airport lounge I thought — this
woman ... (*He stares*) This woman knows how to do it, she's free ...
Maria (*uneasily*) Why you come in house, Joe?
Joe No more Sencorex ... Can't go on. (*Sulkily he stubs his cigarette out and
picks up the ghetto blaster. He stares at Maria then heads for door. He
stops in the sunlit passage, staring straight ahead*) It should be you and me.
Maria Don't say such things, Joe ——
Joe You're driving me crazy.

He turns and watches her shaking her head

I just want you to know how I feel. I can't stop thinking about you — all day, all night.

Maria No, I don't want this — I happy now — I got chance of lifetime.

Joe turns and walks back to her side

Joe It should be you and me ——
Maria I come here for Martin ...
Joe (*close*) He's not up to you ... He's set in his ways, sending for you's the only unusual thing he's ever done — and he was desperate — any woman would have done ——
Maria Don't talk about him Joe, stop this ——
Joe Look at him! He's an old man ——
Maria He's not that old, anyway in Philippines is not sin to be old — old people have respec' not treat like rubbish like in England.
Joe You'll end up looking after an old man on this damn place — and his sister ...

Maria stares

She's ruled him all his life — think she'll go away for your sake? (*He takes her by the arms*) Think Maria, is that what you want?
Maria All I want is to make better life for myself and my family — I want to be material girl living in material world — have life like English woman ... Is it so much to ask?
Joe You could have that with me ... I've got plans, we could go to London — get jobs — really go for it. (*Looking around angrily again*) Really live — one hundred per cent — break the sodding mould ...
Maria Martin do anything for me already. (*She tries to pull free*) Let go me Joe ——
Joe London together, free ——
Maria You drive tractor in London?
Joe Anything, to be with you. (*He pulls her close*) I know you felt the buzz when we danced that night ...
Maria Dance is nothing. I feel nothing.

He kisses her face all over. There is the sound of a vehicle stopping in the yard and doors opening and shutting. Maria struggles

Joe stop this!

Joe bends her back over the end of the table and reaches for his ghetto blaster. He switches it on: "Baby It's You" by the Beatles plays. He straightens and tries to dance with her, crushing her body to his

Joe Listen to it, just listen ... Sha la la la la lah ... It's you, Maria —

Ivy enters and stands in the passage staring

Maria breaks free, pushing Joe away. He notices Ivy and stops the music

Maria Thank you, Joe but I fine as you can see. (*She smiles shakily*)

Martin enters with bags of shopping, shunting Ivy into the room before him

Joe just come in looking for you, Martin.

Martin stares. Ivy moves to table, musing

Martin What's up?
Joe Sencorex run out ...
Martin Again? (*He dumps the bags on the table*) Damn it all, Joe — there must be another drum ...
Joe (*shrugging*) I can't find it.

Martin beckons him towards the back door

They go out, Martin chuntering

Maria meets Ivy's look

Ivy Keeping your options open are you ...
Maria I don't know what you mean.
Ivy He's not much to fall back on.
Maria You talking crazy again.
Ivy Still, only three weeks left of the Fiancé visa — you must be getting a tinge anxious?
Maria You counting days till I go, Ivy?
Ivy (*hissing*) I saw you just now — carrying on — in my kitchen — in the middle of the afternoon ...

Maria giggles with anxiety

You won't be sniggering if I tell Martin. (*She turns away and notices the new cafetière*) What's this?
Maria Is for coffee, like in restaurant.
Ivy More trade goods. (*She stares at Maria*) When he was a little boy Martin saved pennies — big old English pennies in treacle tins — he's always been a good saver. I think those tins are still in the loft — worthless now I expect. (*Pause*) You're going to ruin him.
Maria I don't want these things.
Ivy He's living in a dream about you, (*fiercely*) stupid man ... Well I'll have to break his dream I'm afraid, for his own good.

Maria moves slowly to the sink, grips the cold rim and stares out of window

Maria Do what you like.
Ivy What is your background I wonder ... Nurse?
Maria Hospital secretary not nurse.
Ivy A responsible job even where you come from.
Maria Why are you doing this? I tell truth, I straight as die ...
Ivy I don't think you could lie straight in bed, Miss Bongay. (*She moves closer to Maria like a small witch, sensing her aura, sniffing her out*) I'm very astute about people, it's a family trait — well Martin missed it — but Father was immensely shrewd. If I brought someone home, a friend or colleague, he'd size them up in no time, and advise me. (*She regards Maria*) So demurely dressed on arrival, straight out of the box, dressed to please, Miss Bongay — only something about you didn't ring true.

Maria faces her, her back against the sink, staring

What is it I sense about you. Haven't you ever smelt a fox on your walks — sudden rankness where a fox has crossed your path. It's like that to me — unmistakable.

Maria breaks past and heads for stairs

Yes! Why don't you go and pack your case.

Maria exits upstairs

Ivy stands by the Windsor chair, with a hand on the back runner, reflecting

Martin plods in

Martin If you want summat doing ...

Pause. He looks around, irritated, hot, sensing something. Ivy sits at table, demure but full of power

What was he doing in here?
Ivy (*after a pause*) Nothing.
Martin What was he doing, Ivy?

Ivy stares. Martin picks up plate from the drainer and smashes it on edge of the sink in a fury.

What was he doing!

Black-out

SCENE 6

Late that night

Utter pitch blackness at the window. Looking oddly vulnerable and different with his spectacles on, Martin sits at the desk with Verdi swirling around him, in pool of light from the anglepoise and the glowing computer screen. He takes a swig of Scotch from a glass and stares at the farm accounts — a list of gross margins — on the screen

Maria comes down the stairs in a silk dressing-gown and bare feet. She stops at the bottom and stares at Martin, who notices her and claws the spectacles from his face. She moves to his side stiffly on the cold floor, uncertainly, like a scolded child

Maria You working late, Martin.

Martin half shrugs, his eyes fixed on the screen

I don' know you wear specs, Martin.
Martin You've got a gift for stating the obvious.
Maria What?
Martin Hate myself in 'em ... (*He sighs and toys with his spectacles*) Used
    to need them at school but wouldn't wear 'em ... Used to ask to go to the

toilet so I could peer at what was on the blackboard on my way out — and back ... (*He peers myopically and swivels around in his chair to face her*) Teacher thought I had a weak bladder. (*He swivels his chair back to face the screen and puts the spectacles back on*)

Maria peers at the screen

Maria What are you doing, Martin?
Martin Accounts ... Bloody common market — bureaucracy run riot, more and more forms to fill in, more and more paperwork ... (*Pause*) Can't you sleep?
Maria I come down for drink ...

Martin watches her as she walks to the sink and gets a glass of water

I do nothing to get tired, I can't work in house — I get tired of same walk along road. (*She walks back to him with the glass*)
Martin Should have something on your feet on this floor ... (*He starts to make a note*) Slippers.
Maria (*earnestly*) Martin don't send for slippers. I don't want any more mail order — please?
Martin Just as you like.

She stares at him

I came close to sacking Joe Garbut this afternoon. (*Pause*) You know why, Maria.
Maria It was nothing Martin, believe me.
Martin (*staring at the screen gain*) Joe's not a bad worker most of the time. Used to be as wild as a march hare but he's quietened down lately — still drinks too much but that's his business ... (*He absently taps more information on to the screen — crop analysis, etc.*) He and June have a bairn in care y'know?
Maria Yes?
Martin She's a bit inadequate, he's violent — treats her like a fiddler's bitch to be honest. Without being unfair to the man he's shallow, weak, nasty when drunk ——
Maria Why are you telling me this, Martin?
Martin He's got looks, can't deny that — but he's not a stayer.
Maria He stay here for ten years.
Martin No options, no way out — nothing to make the break for — anyway he's all talk — he needs June for all his bits on the side ...

Maria stares

His other women?

Maria nods sadly

To be blunt he's got the morals of a Moscovy drake — and the appetite.
Latest was wife of landlord at the Wolds Inn ...
Maria (*with her hands in front of her bosom*) That woman ——
Martin Any port in a storm for our Joe.
Maria I'm not interested in what Joe Garbut do, Martin.
Martin No?

He watches her as she heads for the stairs and stops half-way

Maria He try to dance with me that's all — just messing around. I know what
Poison Dwarf tell you but it's not like that.
Martin (*chuckling*) Better not say that in front of her.

She starts to walk back

Maria I don't care what she hear. Finance visa soon up and I go home.

Martin stares, hit

Nobody grope me I don't want to ... (*she checks herself*) Nobody do what
they like with me ... You think I am that kind of woman, Martin?
Martin I'm not saying that ——
Maria What you saying then? You sitting in judgment on me — what I do
wrong?
Martin Nothing, if you say so — I just — wanted to be sure ...
Maria Sure of what, Martin?

He shakes his head, faces front and pecks more figures on to the screen.
Maria stares at them too, by his side

This all about Starfit Farm ... ?

Martin nods, pecking keys, opening the stored heart of the computer to her
intelligent gaze

Martin This is Starfits ... Gross margins, soil and crop analysis, variable costs, fixed costs, net profits ... (*Pause; peck, peck*) Capital investments, labour costs ...

Maria (*softly interested*) Garbut ...

Martin Incomings, outgoings, yearly profits since nineteen twenty-five — I put all Father's notebooks into this, his accounts — this is the one area only I can touch — this and the actual hands-on hard graft ... (*He proudly pecks the keys*) Ivy hasn't a clue about this, it's passed her by. This is mine — every acre, tree, stock and stone practically — Starfits — at my fingertips.

Maria (*staring at the screen*) What this, Martin?

Martin Bank statements ... current account ... investments ... insurances ... All I own and love, Maria.

Maria You love this ...

Martin Why not?

Maria (*moving away slightly, bored*) I dunno. I go back to bed.

Martin (*taking his spectacles off, staring at her*) Why shouldn't I be proud of it? I've made it what it is. It's my baby. Some mornings when I walk out across the yard and see them fields shining and rippling with my crops, I could sing ...

She stares back at him

Surprises you that doesn't it? Hadn't thought of me as a man who might sing. This is me, Maria (*opening his palms to the computer screen*) my life and my work — I increased the yields year by year — I built another silo, another grain drier — bought our own combine and cut out the contractor ... I bought a brand new Volvo one day — I saved and I ordered it and I drove up and saw the shock on Ivy's face at such extravagance. (*He glances at the photo on the dresser*) I felt their shock too, dead as they are I shocked 'em ... I know every inch of this farm, I know every gutter, foxhole, bird's nest and pot hole on every road. I know the soil of every acre — had it analysed — not like him — lifting and sniffing a handful — I've done it properly ... That's the kind of boring chap I am I'm afraid, I like things to be right ...

Maria Why are you telling me this?

Martin This is my work, Maria. This is what I've got to show ...

Maria (*turning away*) I go to bed ——

Martin (*softly, choked*) To offer.

Maria What?

Martin is hunched over the keys, staring at the screen

Martin What am I talking about? Bullshitting myself — I've never sung.
I've done nowt but work around a bloody great aching nothing for years.
(*He wipes the screen*) Nothing. (*He stares at blankness*) Bugger all.

Maria moves to his side and stoops

Maria Martin ... What is matter? Say it ...
Martin (*still staring at the blank screen*) Marry me.

She stares

  Marry me ... Marry me!

Black-out

ACT II

SCENE 1

Monday morning, two weeks later

Rain and grey light on the windows. Maria, dressed for a shopping excursion, sits on the sofa nursing her tape recorder. Ivy clears breakfast pots to the sink, pauses and regards Maria, who feels her gaze and stares back. Ivy continues clearing the pots. There is the sound of the Volvo pulling up outside

Martin enters, rain speckled on his shoulders

Martin Joe not here yet?

Ivy shakes her head

He's getting later every morning. I'll have to have a word with him if he carries on, he'll have to be told. (*He goes towards Maria*) Ready when you are.

Maria puts the tape recorder on the sofa arm and stands, smiling

Maria I ready, Martin.

She picks up her coat and they head for door

Martin See you later ...

Ivy nods, impassive by the sink

Martin and Maria exit through the back door

There is the sound of the car; Ivy listens until it dies away. She walks to the Aga and puts the damp drying cloth she has been using on the rail. She sees the tape recorder, goes to it, picks it up and presses it on

Maria's voice (*from tape recorder*) Is nice little church of All Saints in village with stain' glass windows ... Last thing Mr Stockwell the priest will say is, "May he always honour her and love her as Christ loved his bride the church ... " I have learned my part and banns been read for second time of asking — so soon I be living dream come true. I have found good man who love and respec' me — Martin is my own true love ... Are you happy for me? I only wish you could all be here to see me walk down the aisle with my Martin, my bridegroom on the happy day ...

There is the sound of a vehicle in the yard; Ivy puts the tape recorder down and glances to the door

Joe enters with June in tow, his ghetto blaster silent for once. He is carrying a parcel, an airmail packet, the Yorkshire Post, *and some bills*

Joe Morning, miss! Grand weather for ducks.

Ivy Morning.

Joe (*putting the mail on the table*) Love letters, airmail letters, bills ...

Ivy That Billy Tateson should deliver the mail himself not give it to you at the road end — I've got a good mind to report him.

Joe Ah come on, miss — he's done it for years — saves him half an hour he reckons. Besides, he's getting on.

Ivy He wouldn't have got away with it in my father's day — how are you, June?

June (*glum*) Been worse, how are you?

Ivy Don't ask — (*splaying the fingers of one hand on her lower belly*) grumble grumble ... I'll have to get them seen to one of these days. (*She picks up a parcel, puffs air out of pursed lips, puts it down and checks the bills*)

Joe They've gone off then ...

Ivy You must have passed them.

Joe Yeh, flagged us down to give me a rollicking about being late. I said: "There's nowt much I can do this weather ... " (*He rolls a cigarette*)

June mooches over to a cupboard and drags out the Hoover

Going for the rings are they?

Ivy I wouldn't know. (*She drops the bills*) Bills, bills, bills ...

Joe Chuck 'em, miss, life's too short — that's what I do.

Ivy (*shocked*) You don't ...

She looks to June, who shakes her head

June He would, if I let him.

Ivy picks up the airmail packet and reads the sender's details on the back

Ivy "Zeny Mendoza." The names they give themselves. "Blue Heaven Bar, Ermita." Must be another of her tribe ... (*She stares at Joe and June*) I expected you to be best man, Joe — but do you really want to give her away, June ... ?

June (*shrugging*) She asked ... There's nobody else.

Ivy Everybody's so weak these days. Bosses don't know how to boss, parents don't teach their children the difference between right and wrong — manners are a thing of the past, "respect" is an archaic expression ... I left teaching because the respect had gone — I was beginning to detest the little brats ... I'd had enough. One boy who shall be nameless used to pretend he'd dropped his pencil and crawl about under the desks trying to see up the girls' skirts ...

Joe chuckles

Oh I knew you'd be amused.

June Sure it wasn't him, miss? Sounds like one of his tricks.

Ivy (*shaking her head*) When I scolded him he just stared at me with absolute impudent disregard — and the eyes of a tiny dirty old man. I thought: this child has seen too much — something adult, almost certainly sexual — and it's turned him into this. (*Pause. She turns the airmail packet over in her hands*) Innocent ... How innocent we were.

June You going to the wedding, miss?

Ivy The wedding ... (*Mocking*) Am I going to the wedding? No I am not going to the wedding, June.

June Didn't think you would be.

Ivy How prescient of you. (*Tautly*) I wouldn't go if the alternative was having my entrails drawn out and barbecued on the village green.

Joe and June exchange looks

That woman ... I can't believe how powerless I've been against her. She came into this house like a lamb and I thought: she's nothing, no opposition ... All the years I've been here, all I've done and meant to Martin — given him, given up ... (*She is hit by a memory, staring at the packet*) Why can't he see? They're not a match ——

Joe (*preparing to light a cigarette*) Ah give 'em a chance, miss.

Ivy Yes it's all chance isn't it? Chances and choices and something — arbitrary — ironic — without pity ... (*She drops the packet and gets a grip*) I suppose you've got work to do.

Joe (*holding the lit match*) Bit of maintenance.
Ivy Do it then, before you light that.

Joe blows the match out

You can make a start upstairs, June.
June (*dragging the Hoover towards the stairs*) Martin said give the old
folks' room a going over.

*Ivy stares. Joe grabs the ghetto blaster and heads for the back door, grinning,
but angry*

Joe Get that big double-bed aired!

He goes out

Ivy stares at June

Ivy Their room ... He said to do that?
June Yeah.
Ivy What are things coming to, June ... ?

June stands half-way to the stairs with the Hoover and sniffs lugubriously

Don't sniff, June.
June We been wondering ourselves, like ... I mean she'll soon have a say
won't she, miss? If you see what I mean?
Ivy A say?
June In the running ... We were talking the other night in bed. She — Maria —
she'll be entitled once they're hitched won't she ... Mr and Mrs
Hindshaw ...
Ivy It won't last! (*Spitting it out*) You don't imagine it will last do you? I give
it three months — a year at the outside. They look ridiculous — never been
such an odd couple standing at that altar — he's long past his sell-by date
and as for her ... (*Almost choking with contempt*) He'll sicken of her, he'll
wake up one morning and see her lying there beside him — and contempt
will rise in his mind, disgust ... Be undressed ... (*She stops with a hand to
her throat*) I'm not well, he knows I'm not but he just carries on — fawning
round her ... Cancer of the ovaries kills more than the cervical cancer now
you know? It was in the paper ...

June gapes at her; she notices this and regains control

Wedding? It's a waste of time and money — it'll be over before Christmas ...

June Said that about the War didn't they miss?
Ivy Not even Christmas — harvest? She'll be down the road by harvest.
June With her case full of money an' all ...

Ivy stares

Well I mean, she can't lose either way can she? Once she's got that ring on her finger she's legal isn't she — entitled to half of everything Martin's got?

June goes upstairs with the Hoover

Ivy stands at the head of the table with eyes on the airmail packet, taking in what June has just said. She lifts her gaze to the empty Windsor chair as the Lights fade

Black-out

SCENE 2

Night, ten days later

Classical music from the CD player. There are some crates of drink near the door, for the wedding. Ivy is seated on a chair by the Aga, scissoring rags into box, reducing a shirt to strips. She is very preoccupied. She stops and looks towards the stairs. She thinks, makes a decision and walks to the foot of the stairs, scissors in hand

Ivy (*calling*) Maria! Would you come down please?

Pause

Maria ——

Maria appears at the top of the stairs

I want to speak to you.

She realizes she still has the scissors and puts them on the dresser on her way back to the Aga. Half-way there she turns to watch Maria descending the staircase warily

Maria What you want, Ivy?

Ivy What would it take for you to go?

Maria stares

> What could I do or say or give you just to leave ... I know it's impolite but ... I
> am desperate and I don't want this impossible situation to go on and get
> worse, this hurt ——

Maria Hurt is only because of you — you try to kill our happiness all way
along!

Ivy If that's true it's because I've been the only one seeing clearly round here —
it can only end in tears I promise you ...

Maria (*stunned*) It not end in tears ——

Ivy Mother used to say that. "Father's right, Ivy, it could only end in tears."

Maria What are you talking about?

Ivy I know about these things, Maria ... I had a young man once — we met
at a village dance and he walked me home. Then he went to do his National
Service. (*Smiling almost coyly*) He said he should write and he did — but
Father ... (*swallowing something*) His letters were almost illegible! Child-
ish ... It would have ended in tears — I accepted that.

Maria You asking me to give up? On night before wedding?

*Ivy goes round the sofa to face Maria who starts to back slowly towards
dresser, incredulous and afraid*

Ivy You don't belong here, Maria, you'll never be truly happy here — you
must know that deep down ...

Maria I will be happy. Martin promise me — he move mountain to make
me happy ...

Ivy You don't know him like I do, you haven't even scratched the surface ... As
much as I love him I have to say he can be — irascible ——

Maria stares

> — bad-tempered. I've had my share of miserable days with him I promise
> you — if the weather doesn't suit ... He's limited, Maria, not a match for
> you. Oh I know women marry for all kinds of reasons apart from love but
> Martin is so wrong for you ... I can see this because I'm his sister.

Maria (*coolly*) You love him too much for sister.

Ivy (*shocked*) What ...

Maria You so clever you think you only one watching — but I watch you
back ... You love him more than sister should, more than good for him,
more than natural sister love ...

Ivy Don't you say that to me. (*Hit, livid, she advances on Maria, actually making her hands into claws*) You know nothing about my feelings for my brother, Miss China Doll! I'll break you if you don't go you hear? I'll smash your dreams of avarice ... Coco!

Maria (*with her back to the dresser drawers*) Why you call me that ——

Ivy Suits you ... Coco ... Is Martin going to get his Coco or Joe Garbut as well some nights? Oh there's be plenty of opportunities after a while — I'm sure you've thought of that ... In here the afternoon, in his pickup, in the barn or do you like it alfresco, behind a hedge, (*going into a kind of reverie*) in the plantation, under the sycamores? Those great rustling heads rolling and thrashing against the sky ... Be mine, hold me ...

She comes round and closes stoat-like on Maria, who seems paralysed against the dresser

Oh you've got that, none of them can resist that can they, that's your ace isn't it, that's what blinds them, fuddles their minds — I can't beat that — but it's no foundation for a marriage you greedy little slut!

Pause. Ivy seems utterly in control. Suddenly she smiles and pats Maria on the head

So ... No need for any unpleasantness is there ... Why don't you just trot off home like a good little g ——

Maria has the scissors in her hand and is aiming them threateningly at Ivy's stomach. Ivy stares aghast

You wouldn't ...

Maria I work in slaughterhouse one time — up to elbows in blood and guts all day long — I not afraid of blood.

Ivy You're not civilized ——

Maria You touch me first and last time ... Tomorrow when I come back from church everything will be different. I had enough. No more, "Keep out of kitchen, don't touch this, don't touch that". I know you wipe chairs I sit on! I see you using disinfectant cloth you poison bitch!

She still has the scissors to Ivy's belly, her eyes flashing

But tomorrow is my turn, is turn of little wog woman — little brown woman boss over cold white bitch ...

Ivy (*scared, backing away*) You're unbalanced ——

Maria follows, carving chunks from air between them

Maria Yes! I crazy woman from Manila! If you don't do what I say when I mistress of house I cut your fucking ovary out and have them on toast! On willow pattern plate!

Ivy stumbles to the foot of the stairs and hangs on to the newel post, gasping

Ivy You're mad, absolutely mad — a savage!

Maria brandishes the scissors

Maria Tomorrow kitchen mine, house mine. You think about leaving for good or you be lodger, Ivy Hin'shaw. I Mrs Maria Hin'shaw of Starfit Farm — respeccable woman, good wife ... I have security for once in life, I take no shit from nobody, no more humiliation! (*Softer*) I be what I want to be — or you never sleep safe in bed again ...

Ivy starts to haul herself upstairs. There is the sound of a vehicle entering and stopping in the yard. Doors slam. Maria heads for the dresser. Martin, Joe and June sing as they move to the house: "Get Me to the Church on Time". They sing "for Pete's sake", not "for God's sake"

   They three of them enter

Joe stands grinning with Martin, almost comatose, hanging around his shoulders. June, impassive, is just behind, holding the ghetto blaster. Maria slips the scissors back into the drawer

Joe Maria ... Ivy ... we're back!

He drops Martin on to the sofa and heads for the stairs

   Ivy Hindshaw come on down — let's party!

Joe pulls Ivy towards the table, but she shakes his hand off. He goes off around the kitchen in search of more drink. He finds a bottle from some crates for the wedding. Ivy goes to Martin's side

Ivy You shouldn't have got him into this state. He's not used to drink ...

She lifts his glazed features up then lets go

Martin look at you ...

He struggles, trying to focus

I'm here, Martin.
Martin Maria ...
Maria (*approaching*) Here I am, Martin ...
Martin (*grabbing her hand*) You all right my love?
Maria I fine, Martin, things getting better all time.
Martin (*slurring*) Told you, told you they would did' I ... Ivy's not such a
bad old stick are you, Ivy?

Ivy stares at him

Cheer up for God's sake — have some generosity ... It's a wedding not a
funeral.
June They were staggering about on the village green, thought I'd better
bring them back ...
Martin Where's the Volvo, Joe?
Joe (*with an open bottle*) Wide-eyed and legless — I've gone and done it
again! Don't worry about the tank, Martin, we'll find it in the morning ...

Martin sings a slurring dirge: "I'm Getting Married in the Morning"

Martin ... ding dong the bells, the bells ——
Joe (*Quasimodo impression*) The bells, the bells Maria ——
Ivy Stop this!

They stop. Joe swigs from the bottle at the table end

Maria So this is English stag night? It one stupid idea.

She helps Martin to his feet. June puts the ghetto blaster on the dresser

Let's get him to bed or he fit for nothing in morning.
Joe (*laughing*) Or evening!
June Belt up, you!

*June helps Maria take Martin towards the stairs. Ivy takes his arm from
Maria*

Ivy I'll see to him — June?

Maria seems about to protest

   I'll put him to bed tonight.

She and June take Martin upstairs

Maria turns to see Joe regarding her, no longer as drunk as he seemed

Joe You're going through with it then.
Maria You're not so drunk, Joe Garbut.
Joe (*shrugging*) Just keeping the old lad company. Can't seem to get drunk
   any more — I just get miserable.
Maria (*staring at the floor*) I miserable ... I bad woman, not fit for Martin's
   wife.
Joe He's talked about you all night, drooling on about you. "My Maria", he
   says, "isn't she lovely, Joe lad, isn't she something ... " I felt like cracking
   him (*staring at her*) and dumping him in the pond. I can do things like that —
   things other people only talk about then shove away — I can do 'em. I'm
   different. (*He sits on the end of the table and stares at her*) We're different
   ... I admire you. I didn't think you'd go for it but you have — you've
   cracked it ... Mrs Maria Hindshaw, partner in the firm, joint account — just
   like a true romance comic — with a wedding on the last page. Bells ringing.
   Heaven coming down with the confetti. (*He sings suddenly, hit, hard-
   edged; a parody of Meat Loaf's "Heaven Can Wait". He stops. Pause*) I'm
   glad for you.
Maria Really, Joe?

He sings again, brutally, bitterly. He pauses, and gives her a pained stare

Joe What do you want, Maria?
Maria What I going to get, someone who love and respec' me, who treat me
   like a person in equal relationship, who see me like real woman not fantasy —
   good, kind man ...
Joe You bought the whole package didn't you. This is old Martin you're
   talking about?
Maria I told you — age don't matter. I had young men — every time I follow
   eyes and heart I get hurt bad. This time I go with head and brain — maybe
   I get lucky.
Joe What about me ...

Maria Tomorrow Martin is my husband, it all arranged — he do anything
to make me happy.

Joe I hope you're right. (*He stands up*) I think he'll clip your wings ... I've
realized something watching you two — people from different countries
can't see each other properly; he thinks you're this exotic bird he's got to
have — Bird of Paradise — and you think he's a lot more than he is —
decent bloke, a good catch. (*He laughs*) He's a bloody joke round here.
(*"Mooing" it*) Old Ma-a-a-rtin ...

Maria Martin is OK ——

Joe (*moving closer*) You don't know him ... I've seen him break things, bash
things to bits like a loony ——

Maria I give him my word ——

Joe You're all the talk in the pub ... They think you're going after this brass
and he's fallen for the obvious. "How's Suzie Wong?" they ask me "You
slipping her a length an' all, Joe?"

Maria I don't care about dirty minds ——

Joe (*close*) "Three in a bed at Starfits is it, Joe?" I nearly punched this fat git
out one night over you ...

Maria I don't care what they say ——

Joe (*singing tensely at her*) I don't care what they say — about you — cheat
cheat — sha la la la la ...

Maria You singer as well, Garbut? I just carn understand why you not
famous ——

Joe Famous ... (*He shrugs*) Never expected famous, but like Poison Ivy used
to put on my reports, "Should have done better ... "

Maria Why didn't you then?

Joe Drifted it ... Frittered it away for laughs and (*with the bottle*) this stuff ... Easy-
going Joe, Mr Cool — good for a laugh, one of the lads, pub man ... Bairned
a stupid little heifer one night and married her — drifted into that — when
I went to the church you'll be in tomorrow I didn't want any of it. Just went
along with it — still half cut ... Automatic pilot right up to the altar ...
(*Pause*) When they took the kid I thought — this is my chance. I'll go —
but I didn't — why bother? (*He stares at her, grins in self mockery and
sings a line from "Maria"*)

Maria You marry a girl named June ——

Joe Oh yeah, June — the embarrassment ... She bores me rigid — but can
I leave the stupid cow? (*He stares. Pause*) I wanted you. Everything you
are I wanted.

Maria (*glancing to the stairs*) Don't do this, Joe ——

He takes her in his arms

Joe Say you feel nothing for me ... Tell me you haven't thought about being with me in any way — for one minute of any day — and I'll let you go ... Maria?
Maria Don't do this to me please ——
Joe I know you were meant to be with me ——
Maria I don't want this ——

He tries to kiss her, but her twisting face is elusive

Joe I'll take you away, you're too good for him, it's all wrong, it's a travesty ——

He holds her fighting body

Stop fighting me you bitch ——
Maria Asshole! (*Suddenly she goes limp as a doll in his arms*) OK you wanna fuck. Where you want me — floor? Table end maybe like in "Postman Always Ring Twice"? We get it over then maybe you leave me alone.

Joe releases her, shocked

Joe I don't want it like that ——
Maria So why you come pawing me, what else you want? You know I getting married tomorrow and still you think you can do this — you think you can have me first and brag about it in pub maybe?

Joe stares

You men are all the same, you get fantasy (*drilling her temple with a finger*) in here and some drink and think it can be done no problem!

June descends the stairs slowly, listening

All my life men come after me like dogs, since I young girl men look at me as if I something good to eat, something on butcher's slab, not person at all. Always saying things, I beautiful, I this, I that — never leave me alone, never ask how I feel. Sometimes I wish I ugly as sin — ugly woman nobody want!

Joe starts towards her then notices June and stops

Don't come near me ... I don't want to be touched. I say this for Martin, he
never touch me—he never take liberties ... (*She follows Joe's gaze to June*)
June ... Is Martin OK?
June Senseless ... Lord knows what he'll be like in the morning.
Maria He make it all right.

June stares at Joe as she walks past to the door

June God you're predictable ... Disgusting pig!

Joe glares at her and goes out

June regards Maria without animosity

He's never grown up. Isn't that strange—and it doesn't seem to matter for
a man. Always a greedy grabbing child — and some woman will always
let him have whatever he wants ... (*She moves to the dresser and runs a
finger along the top of the ghetto blaster*) You shouldn't be here tonight you
know. Martin shouldn't see you — it's bad luck.
Maria We get back from church tomorrow. Not need luck.
June I thought you'd be dead superstitious — just shows. (*She shakes her
head and grins*) You've got some balls, Maria.
Maria I hope not or Martin making big mistake.

*They giggle together and almost touch. June sits on a chair at the table and
lights a cigarette*

June I mean, you've cracked it — fallen on your feet.
Maria Fallen on feet?
June Marrying Martin. You'll never want again if you play your cards right.
Maria (*like a mantra*) Never want again.
June (*with a shrewish accent*) "She's seen her way in theer" — that's what
the old biddies are saying — "She'll fleece him". (*Pause*) Wish I had your
luck and your nerves. You saw what you wanted and went for it. Us women
have to take our chances.
Maria Maybe your luck change, June.
June Don't deserve any ... It's bloody murder without my little girl, Maria.
She's not here but she's with me all the time ... (*She closes her eyes*) I close
my eyes and her face floats up. First thing in the morning, last thing at night ...
Maria (*hit, desperate to help*) Don't worry about your job anyway, I still
need cleaner here.

June turns sub-zero, gets up and heads for the door

June Well! That's all right then isn't it! (*She does a mock curtsy by the door*)
    See you in the morning, Mrs Hindshaw!
Maria (*shocked*) No don't call me that yet ——
June Good-night!

   June storms out

Maria stands alone C, *diminished and unsure. She puts her hand to her face
like a little girl*

Maria (*like a supplicant*) Mama ... Is going to be OK ... I am doing right thing,
    Mama ... Is what I been waiting for .... (*A bit of dialogue in Filipino*) It just
    never ... (*She starts to break up*) Mama? (*She gives a cry for reassurance*)

Lights fade to Black-out

SCENE 3

The next morning

*There is sunshine in the open doorway and the faint sound of bells pealing
across the wolds. Ivy, in her usual pinny and frock, sits at the table staring
towards the door. The ghetto blaster is at her elbow. She looks serene,
decided*

*After a moment Martin comes slowly down stairs looking hungover but smart
in a suit, which is slightly too youthful for him. He goes to the sink, bends over
and drinks straight from the tap. Ivy regards him*

Ivy You look like something out of Burton's window ... In nineteen forty-
    five ...

Martin stands and takes it. He checks his watch

  Getting anxious?
Martin We've got to be there in thirty minutes.
Ivy And they've just had the church roof repaired ——
Martin Don't, Ivy ——
Ivy (*sharp*) You can't change Father's will you realize that? I've checked
    with them about that.

Martin (*pained*) Why would I ... You'll get everything you're entitled to. (*He regards her and sighs*) Do you have to be like this?

Ivy If you don't change your mind — yes I do.

Martin sighs

Don't sigh, Martin.

Martin You could attend the service, it'd mean at lot to us.

Ivy (*smiling*) Such an innocent you are, Martin — you haven't changed one iota.

Martin You're perfect I suppose.

Ivy I have many faults but being a hypocrite is not one of them — which is why I shall not be present at this charade ...

There is the sound of a vehicle approaching. Martin goes to the window

Martin It's them, they're here ...

Ivy sits motionless as doors slam in the yard. Martin goes to the foot of the stairs and shouts "Maria!" up towards the door as:

Joe and June enter in their wedding outfits — suit with buttonhole and summer frock. Joe carries buttonholes and June is smiling; they are both putting a good face on it

Glad to see you two, I was getting edgy.

Joe Take it easy, boss, it's not as if the bride might not turn up ... Morning. Ivy ...

Ivy nods and gets up and wanders to the sink area

Stand still a minute.

Joe pins the buttonhole on Martin's lapel

Nice flute — demob was it?

Martin (*cheered by their presence*) Cheeky sod — Maria chose it out of catalogue.

Joe looks inside the suit for the label

Joe Habitat?

June laughs rather too long and loud

   She's been at the sherry.
Martin Fits all right doesn't it? I thought it was a good fit considering.
June (*fixing her buttonhole*) You look very nice, Martin.
Joe Every inch the bridegroom ... (*He takes a half bottle of Scotch from his
   pocket*) Feel like a swift one? Steady the nerves.

Martin groans and shakes his head. Joe swigs from the bottle and gasps

Joe Hair of the scabby dog ... can't beat it.

He stares to the stairs as:

   *Maria descends the stairs holding a small bouquet. She looks stunning in
   an olive shantung dress and hat. The distant bells are pealing in singles
   now, faintly dying*

   (*Singing the wedding march*) Dum dum da dum ...

*They all stare. Ivy turns away to the sink and window, hit. Martin meets Maria
at the foot of the stairs*

Martin Maria ...
June You look fantastic, Maria.

*She crosses room and kisses Maria, who laughs with pleasure and turns to
the gobstruck Martin*

Maria Am I still on sale or return, Martin?
Martin You're approved ...

*He takes her in his arms and tries to kiss her but she eludes him, twisting away
with a giggle*

Maria Not smudge lipstick, Martin! Kiss bride after vows not before!

Jokingly, Joe pursues Maria

Joe Best man has his privileges dun' he?

June shields the giggling Maria

June After the ceremony, greedy guts — and put your buttonhole on ... Come here.

Joe stands still as June fixes his carnation in place, their faces close

This is all wrong — leaving the house with bride. It's all wrong ——
Ivy Yes it is ...

They stare at her, silhouetted by the sunshine pouring through the window

Terribly wrong.

She crosses room and goes briskly upstairs

Pause

Martin Got the ring, Joe lad?
Joe Course I have. (*He pats his pockets with increasing mock panic, grins and pulls out a roll of white ribbon*) Damn, this should be on limo ...
Martin Does it matter?

He notices Maria's expression

Yeah, let's do it right — I'll give you a hand.

They go out

June and Maria stand together. Maria looks downed

June Take no notice of her.
Maria I never come across such a cold bitch.
June She's a Hindshaw ... (*She realizes what she's said and grimaces*)

Maria walks to the door and looks out, watching the men. June watches her

I expect Joe tried his luck before last night?

Maria turns and stares at her

It's all right, don't think you're anything special that's all. I wouldn't trust him with that yard broom ... Anything with hairs on it ...

Maria I don't understand ...

June I was seventeen when we met ... He was footballing for Duggleby and
   I had a right pash on him.

Maria Pash?

June Passion ... Only used to go to matches to see him in his strip. He took
   a corner right where I was standing with me mates — winked at me and
   said, "What you doing tonight then?"

Maria listens. The men laugh, off

   Next thing I knew I was up stick.

Maria frowns

   Pregnant ...

Maria nods sadly

   Knew I would be minute he shot his load ... Fated I was ...

Maria You still love Joe?

June After ten years of him — drinking, gambling and screwing around?
   (*Pause*) Yeah.

They laugh together softly, shortly

   You must think me a right fool.

Maria stares back out into the yard

Maria Everybody somebody's fool, June ...

June Bloody man ... (*Thinking back*) When he rolled off me in the back of
   his van the first time I thought, I've got him, he'll love me forever for this,
   but when he lit a cig and glanced at me I could see he just wanted to be off.
   He was all done — mission accomplished — just another silly little slag
   who'd opened her legs ... Don't suppose you know what I mean, Maria?

Maria All women know that sometime ... But good loving man does exist,
   June — I got to believe that.

Ivy comes down the stairs with something in her hand, musing

Joe and Martin lumber back in

Joe All right! All aboard for All Saints!
Martin We should be on our way.

A bit of confusion occurs in the doorway. Ivy reaches the foot of the stairs. It is a cassette tape she is carrying. Joe raises his arms

Joe Whoa! It's very simple, June and the bride follow me and the groom — just to let us get into church first ... Sort yourselves out!

June crooks an arm and Maria takes it, giggling. Joe and Martin fall in behind, Martin tugs at his tight collar. Ivy clicks the cassette tape into the ghetto blaster and the sound makes them all look back into the room

Joe What's this, Miss Hindshaw — going to play us out?
Ivy Martin, I think you should hear this before you go.
Martin (*angry*) We haven't time, Ivy ——
Ivy I've wrestled with it for days but I think it has to be done — it is my duty.
Joe It'll have to wait till we get back ——
Martin For God's sake, Ivy what's it about?
Ivy (*staring at Maria*) Trust, I think ... Honesty and inheritance — the wishes of the dead ... Father and Mother have been so strong with me lately — you won't have felt them but I have ... I know ...
Maria (*sensing it*) Don't listen to her, Martin — she's just trying to stop us. (*She pulls him towards the sunny doorway*) Let's go to church please?

Martin pauses, torn. Ivy stabs the play button and the room is swamped with the sounds of Subic City street life: revving jeeps, etc. It is an alien, exotic, very loud cacophony. Zeny's voice comes excitedly to the fore

Zeny's voice Hi, Coco! It wonderful to talk to you like this! We miss you so much it is boring here now and nobody make us laugh or try to help us. The guys are the same crazy assholes ... Imelda has baby son, Mary Ann is fucked up on speed ... and I worried Paula has got HIV — she gone very thin and say nothing all time ... The new DJ plays shit music. (*She giggles. Other female Filipino voices chatter and shout: "Hi Coco! We love you!", etc.*) We so happy you going to be married Coco and looking forward to wedding photos! We so happy for you but sad for ourselves ... You so lucky living in material world! Send us all rich Englishmen like Martin eh — we do anything for man like that!
Maria (*in horror and anger*) This is my mail, this must be sent to me ——

She tries to reach Ivy and the ghetto blaster but Martin keeps hold of her hand

Martin let me go!

Martin holds on, aghast, stubborn

Don't listen to this ...

She is stilled as Martinez' voice from the tape fills the room like that of some jolly green American giant

Martinez' voice Coco! It's Chuck baby here!

Maria stands like a woman in a nightmare. Martin drops her hand

I'm happy for you too honey though kinda sore about you taking off for the UK while the *Saratoga* was at sea ... Still, I figure the only way to forget one sweet LBFM is in the arms of another — right honey? (*From the tape, the sound of a woman giggling and squealing as if being goosed*) Things are kinda quiet in Subic City now we're pulling out but anyway I ain't going back to the US of A — nosir I'm going into business right here ... I'm gonna open up Blue Heaven Bar *Two* — sounds really wild huh? I figure all kinds of tourists want to meet LBFMs — so if you get tired of that old limey sugar daddy, your job's waiting for you back here, any time ... (*His voice slurs with drink and desire*) I'll never forget you, Coco honey — you still the best goddamn LBFM I ever had ... I'm keeping a fatherly eye on Donna, and I'm still horny for you Coco — still the same ole Chuck, so horny even the crack of dawn ain't safe! (*He laughs*)

Maria gives a strangled cry and rushes to the ghetto blaster, scattering her bouquet. She pushes Ivy aside and claws the cassette from the machine. She drops it to the floor and stamps on it, then stands shaking, her face in her hands

Joe (*staring*) Shore time sailor's whore ...

Martin goes towards her

Martin Coco ——
Maria Not Coco! I Maria ——
Ivy A bar-girl ——
Maria Yes I bar-girl! (*Facing them all*) I lose job at hospital because boss

trying to screw me all time, sexual harassment you call it here — here you take man to court — in Manila fat slob think he can shove hand up skirt any time he like — put your hand on his dick — leave filthy pictures in tray ... So I leave, I try for other jobs but he give me bad name and no reference ... I see family going downhill — children getting food from bins behind Blue Heaven Bar ... One day I trying to stop them when Chinese owner come out and offer me job ... I am bar-girl to support my family — since Father die I am all they have — Mama, Nana, eight little ones ... (*She breaks up at the thought of them*) Donna my little girl, I love her so much I do anything — I want her to have decent life ——

Ivy She's got a daughter would you believe ——

Maria (*to Martin*) I was going to tell you in good time ——

Ivy When she'd got the ring on her finger ——

Maria I was going to ask if I could bring her to Starfits ——

Ivy puffs out incredulous air. Maria turns on her

I am not ashamed!

Martin Were you and that — (*he looks to the ghetto blaster*) cowboy married?

Maria No! I hate him ... Martinez cruel son of bitch who think he own me — no good for husband no good for father — only good for fucking brains out ——

Ivy gasps

He like fat Manaboas monkey — fuck anything that move. (*She holds her mouth, horrified*) Sorry for bad words, sorry I not tell truth — sorry, Martin ...

Martin stands shocked, trying to absorb this

You must understand how it is for many Filipino woman ... We got nothing, even father and mother sorry we not born sons — our own men sell us all time, fuck us all time, fuck us younger and younger. My Nana tell me about Japanese occupation — Filipino women in huts in jungle chained to beds like animal for foreigners to fuck — years ago ... Best of women going into cities to be fucked, infected — whole country fucked up by Yanks and other foreigners ... But I not bad woman — I still your Maria ... (*Pause*) Martin ...

Martin I don't know what to say.

Ivy Thank God for the tape I say — soiled goods, brother — send her back ...

Maria Martin ... Stand by me ... Or I think I go crazy ——

Joe suddenly starts rapping like a crazed robot, full of pain, singing "Return to Sender". When he reaches the line "No such zone", June slaps his face, stopping him

June Shut up you!

Joe stands shocked. Pause

Martin LBFM ... What is that?
Maria (*hit*) Is nothing, I dunno what it mean — some crazy thing Martinez dream up — nothing important ...
Ivy An acronym ... Like HIV ... VD ... AIDS ... count your blessings, brother ...
Martin (*hit*) He said ... you were his LBFM — best ever ...
Maria It no matter! (*Backing towards the stairs*) You give me no chance, you don't care what I trying to do — raise standard of life — not one of you care. (*Pointing to Ivy*) You never be sister to me, you got no love ——
Joe Maria ——
Maria Don't waste breath, Joe — men just assholes, same all over world ——
Joe I meant what I said ——
Maria (*shaking her head*) You want Coco not Maria — always smiling Coco, always available — not real Maria with needs of her own. You got no real love for woman, no tender care and respec' — no understanding ... (*She shouts*) I not whore! (*Sadly, softly*) I sister, mother, friend ... I daughter ... I person ... (*She stands by the newel post as the tears come. She rubs her eyes childishly*) Mama, I so sorry ... I lose everything ...

Joe starts towards Maria. But he is blocked by Martin's outflung arm. They wrestle and Joe is flung to the floor

Martin Keep out of this ——
Joe I still love you like I said ——
Maria I never fall in love again.
Joe I still want you ——
Maria I don't want no part of your crazy love. (*Suddenly in control of herself, terribly hit but resilient and courageous. She's a survivor*) What about you, Martin?
Martin (*tersely*) The offer still stands.

Maria shakes her head and starts up stairs

Joe Maria ...
Maria (*pausing, smiling sadly*) You both so romantic — Mister Bigshot DJ ...
Mister Mail Order Man ... You never have respec' for me now. It always
coming into your mind I second-hand woman — and I not always be
beautiful. Some day I am slant-eyed old Chink woman you not want to take
anywhere ... (*She looks down on them and says with weary finality*) You
not want LBFM for wife. You not want Little Brown Fucking Machine.

Ivy gasps

Maria exits upstairs without looking back

*Martin moves to the end of the table like a man in a trance of pain and
disbelief. Joe glares around, angry and devastated, out of his depth. He takes
an angry lunge towards Martin's back but June intercepts*

*She bundles him off out into the sunny yard where he shouts something
furious and unintelligible. She shrieks back "Leave it!", and shouts
something unintelligible herself*

*There is the sound of their vehicle leaving. Ivy regards Martin from her chair,
then gets up and goes towards the stairs. She pauses and looks at him. Their
stares lock as the Lights begin to fade*

Black-out

SCENE 4

Mid-afternoon the same day

*Martin sits in his father's chair. He is still in his wedding suit. There is a bottle
of Scotch and a glass at his elbow. Verdi's* Requiem *swirls around room*

*Maria comes downstairs, dressed for a journey, carrying her case. Martin
watches her walk towards the door*

Martin I said I'd run you down.
Maria I order taxi — it quicker.
Martin (*pained*) What will you do?
Maria I find work somewhere, send for Donna maybe. Somewhere, a place
for us. (*She stares at him, then smiles*) Goodbye, Martin, no hard feeling ...

Martin You don't have to go.
Maria I think so.
Martin Why didn't you tell me?
Maria I come here to start new life, leave all old crap behind ... You never
   sent for bar-girl — tell truth, Martin!
Martin (*choked*) I still want you ...
Maria Want maybe, not love ——
Martin Love, yes ——
Maria But I don't love you, Martin —

He stares, hit. There is the sound of a taxi outside. A horn blows

Just one of those things — if I don't love at first sight I never love — it just
not there ... I cry for long time on my bed, Martin and no-one come to me.
I go through all my shit life and I think I am nothing but LBFM like
Martinez say. Then I get up and have long bath in all soap and oil I got —
I feel clean inside and I know it not my fault. I did what I had to do at time
and that end of story ... It way of world, Martin, and way of men ... Men
have lost spirit of good, of nature — they destroying all beauty in world if
they go on — beauty of tree, sea, mountain, forest — and women ... We
frighten men I think so they got to destroy, make us nothing but whores ...
Make us ugly animals like themselves — I think they hate their mothers
so they killing her in beauty of women and innocence of children ... When
Mother Earth herself is raped and dead they maybe be satisfied ... They sit
beside her and weep then. They show spirit too late.

She stops as:

Ivy comes down the stairs slowly

But I am me, Martin, I am person — own woman who belong to no-one
but herself ... I be OK, I will survive. (*She stares across the room at Ivy,
head up, proud*) You got what you want, Ivy eh — you won like always.
But I still rather be me than you — I sorry for you!

She moves along the passage and out into the sunlight

*Martin turns his head towards the sunny window but does not get up. He
slumps slightly into his chair. Ivy walks to the dresser and stands between it
and the table*

Ivy You'll thank me in time ...

Martin lifts his head slowly to stare at her

You had to be brought to your senses. I believe that tape was meant to fall into my hands.

Martin Maybe ... (*Pause*) And maybe you were right to tell me but I'll never thank you for it.

Ivy You'd rather I let you marry (*with a glance to the door*) that?

Martin stares at her

Martin I never realized ... Been so close to you for so long I couldn't see it. You've got something lacking, sister — a black hole where something should be — compassion, generosity of spirit ... Pity ...

Ivy (*hit*) I've given you my life ——

Martin Shouldn't have. Not your place. Look what you've made of us — (*gesturing across them*) fallow land ... Set aside ... (*With pained dignity*) My first real chance ... (*he gives a short, severing gesture*) How could you ...?

Ivy turns to the wedding photo

Ivy For your own good! Father would approve, he would understand ——

Martin Our Father! That moralizing old bastard! Why do you go on loving him after what he did to you? (*He stares, pauses*) I do remember you know.

Ivy I don't know what you mean ——

Martin Father's Little Treasure, Mother's Little Helper — bringing him his slippers and his paper, running to fetch the mail ... Always trying to please ... Even after that — poor lovelorn sod ...

Ivy What are you talking about? This is silly talk ——

Martin He walked you home from the Saturday night bus didn't he? Bit of a snog by the yard gate — under the sycamores — in his khaki ...

Ivy We kissed — I didn't encourage him. What a vulgar expression ... "Bit of a snog", really ..

Martin Like BURMA on the back of a letter B-U-R-M-A ... What a pity, the old man took to him. He was smart, he had manners — his family weren't short of a bob or two — but it was a mistake — BURMA ... On the back of a bluey from — Cyprus was it — or Aden?

Ivy Irrelevant, ancient history — it doesn't matter ... He had every right!

Martin To open someone else's letter ... Private, secret, love letter — sitting here like God and reading it aloud — a man's intimate words — till you cried and ran to your room and I walked blazing into that yard ... Impotent as usual before him — but wanting him dead as a bloody hammer ... Wanting to hurt him so bad ——

Ivy (*holding on to the back of a chair*) No more, Martin, you know I'm not well ——

Martin (*calmly*) You'll see me out, Ivy ...

Ivy I must go and have a lie down. (*She turns and walks towards the foot of the stairs*)

Martin (*watching her go*) "Sweetheart", he called you. "My sweet love". "I can't wait to feel you in my arms again" ——

Ivy Enough ——

Martin Then the bit that made the old tyrant's eyes pop — BURMA ... "By the way BURMA means ——"

Ivy starts up the stairs as if to escape his words

(*Following her*) I was only a kid, Ivy but it stirred me when I thought about it — listening to you sobbing in your bed next door — I thought it was a wonderful thing to ask for!

Ivy flees off through the door on the landing

(*Martin stands at top of stairs, shouting after her*) — to wait for and long for and dream about ... BURMA ... "Be Undressed and Ready My Angel". ...

There is a passionate but furious shout at the door. Martin turns at the sound of a vehicle pulling into the yard. As the doors slam shut, he looks towards the door, hoping for a moment. The look disappears as:

Joe enters in a wary but determined manner. He notices Martin

Joe Martin ... (*He glances towards the stairs*)

Martin She's gone.

Pause. Joe moves towards the dresser

What did you want?

Joe (*laying hold of the ghetto blaster*) Just this ——

Martin With her ...

Joe regards him

Joe What did you?

Pause. Joe heads for the door with his ghetto blaster

Martin Did you finish that flap t'other day?
Joe (*pausing, facing the door*) All but top side ——
Martin Better crack on in morning then — rain's forecast.

Joe nods and goes out

There is the sound of his vehicle leaving. The light in the yard and at the window changes to evening red and gold, and then even darker. Martin closes the door and goes into the office area. He presses the CD and we hear something poignant, plangent. He bends to insert a tape into the VCR. He takes the remote control to his father's chair and sits down and pours a scotch into the glass. The video begins — there is the sound of gibbering Filipino females. He fast forwards to the bit where Maria speaks

Maria's voice My name is Maria Bongay, I am twenty-six years old and looking for someone to love and respec' me ... (*She giggles; she is charming, inimitable*)

Martin rewinds and plays it again

My name is Maria Bongay, I am twenty-six years old and looking for someone to love and respec' me ... (*The same giggle*)

Martin rewinds and plays it again

My name is Maria Bongay, I am twenty-six years old and looking for someone to love and respec' me ... (*The same giggle*)

Martin is thinking, lost in reverie, summoning up the essence of it all. He stops the tape and puts the control on the top of the TV. The music swirls around the room as he walks to the door and looks across the yard. He stands in the doorframe in the decaying light, hurt but somehow resolute, changed for the better despite his pain

Fade to Black-out

FURNITURE AND PROPERTY LIST

ACT I
Scene 1

On stage: Oak dresser. *On it:* photographs, wedding photograph, Willow pattern
china on racks
Work boots
Clothes hanging on pegs
Desk. *On it:* farm computer and monitor
Swivel chair
Anglepoise lamp
CD player, CDs in record stackers
Table and chairs, including Windsor chair. *On table: Yorkshire Post,*
tea-cup
TV, video cassette recorder and tapes on rack, including one tape from
the "Filipino Friendship Agency"
Sofa
Calendar of Yorkshire views
Farming weeklies, mail order catalogues
In kitchen area: crockery, cutlery, draining board, wipes, etc.

Off stage: Rattan case (**Joe**)

Personal: **Martin**: watch
Maria: sunglasses

Scene 2

Strike: *Yorkshire Post*

Set: Mug of tea, breakfast plate on table (**Martin, Ivy**)
Rattan case near doorway

Off stage: Bunch of common grasses (**Maria**)
Ghetto blaster, bills (**Joe**)
Polish and duster (**June**)

Scene 3

Strike: Bills
Bunch of common grasses

| *Set:* | Tin containing sandwiches (**Joe**) |
| | Ghetto blaster (**Joe**) |

| *Off stage:* | Shopping bags. *In one:* cassette and tape recorder with microphone for Maria (**Martin**) |

| *Personal:* | **Joe**: cigarettes, matches |
| | **June**: cigarettes, lighter, handbag |

SCENE 4

| *Strike:* | Shopping bags |

| *Set:* | Chairs on top of table |

| *Personal:* | **June**: watch |
| | **Maria:** handbag |

SCENE 5

| *Strike:* | Ghetto blaster |

Set:	Mail order acquisitions on table; cafetière, slow cooker, toaster
	Tape recorder and tapes (**Maria**)
	Plate at sink (**Martin**)

| *Off stage:* | Ghetto blaster (**Joe**) |
| | Shopping bags (**Martin**) |

| *Personal:* | **Joe**: filthy paper mask, cigarettes, matches |

SCENE 6

| *Strike:* | Shopping bags |
| | Ghetto blaster |

| *Set:* | Scotch, glass on desk (**Martin**) |
| | Glass near sink (**Maria**) |

| *Personal:* | **Martin**: spectacles |

ACT II
SCENE 1

On stage:	Tape recorder (**Maria**)
	Breakfast pots, etc., drying cloth (**Ivy**)
	Hoover (in cupboard) (**June**)

Off stage: Parcel, airmail packet, *Yorkshire Post*, bills, ghetto blaster (**Joe**)

Personal: **Joe**: cigarettes, lighter

SCENE 2

Strike: Parcel
Airmail packet
Yorkshire Post
Bills
Ghetto blaster

Set: Scissors, shirt for rags, box (**Ivy**)
Crates of drink with one bottle for Joe

Off stage: Ghetto blaster (**June**)

SCENE 3

Strike: Scissors, shirt, box

Set: Ghetto blaster from dresser to table

Off stage: Carnation buttonholes (**Joe**)
Bouquet (**Maria**)
Cassette tape (**Ivy**)

Personal: **Martin**: watch
Joe: long white ribbon

SCENE 4

Set: Scotch and glass (**Martin**)

Off stage: Case (**Maria**)

LIGHTING PLOT

1 interior. The same throughout
Practical fittings required: light effect from TV, computer monitor, anglepoise lamp

ACT I, SCENE 1

To open: Full interior lighting; afternoon effect through doors and window

Cue 1   **Martin** presses the play button on the VCR control   (Page 4)
             TV effect for duration of video

Cue 2   **Martin** presses pause   (Page 5)
             The screen light flickers

Cue 3   **Martin** flicks VCR off   (Page 5)
             All TV effects cease

Cue 4   **Martin** looks up the length of the table   (Page 11)
             Black-out

ACT I, SCENE 2

To open: Full interior lighting: sunny morning effect through window, etc.

Cue 5   **Martin** stands defiantly   (Page 18)
             Black-out

ACT I, SCENE 3

To open: Full interior lighting: midday effect through window, etc.

Cue 6   **Ivy** stands by her father's chair after **Martin**'s exit   (Page 26)
             Fade to black-out

ACT I, SCENE 4

To open: Dim interior lighting, night effect outside

Cue 7   **Martin** bows his head down over the CD player   (Page 34)
             Fade to black-out

ACT I, SCENE 5

To open: Full interior lighting; mid-afternoon sunshine effect outside

Cue 8   **Martin**: "What was he doing!"   (Page 40)
        Black-out

ACT I, SCENE 6

To open: Dim interior lighting, anglepoise on, computer lights on, black outside

Cue 9   **Martin**: "Marry me ... marry me!"   (Page 44)
        Black-out

ACT II, SCENE 1

To open: Full interior lighting; grey light and rain effect outside

Cue 10   **Ivy** lifts her gaze to the empty Windsor chair   (Page 49)
        Fade to black-out

ACT II, SCENE 2

To open: Full interior lighting; night effect outside

Cue 11   **Maria** gives a cry for reassurance   (Page 58)
        Fade to black-out

ACT II, SCENE 3

To open: Full interior lighting; morning sunshine effect outside

Cue 12   **Ivy** and **Martin** lock stares   (Page 67)
        Fade to black-out

ACT II, SCENE 4

To open: Full interior lighting; mid-afternoon sunshine effect outside

Cue 13   The sound of **Joe**'s vehicle leaving   (Page 71)
        Change outside light to evening red/gold, then darker

Cue 14   **Martin** plays video   (Page 71)
        Flicker effect from TV on and off as per p. 71

Cue 15   **Martin** stops the video   (Page 71)
        All TV effects cease

Cue 16   **Martin** stands, resolute, near the doorway   (Page 71)
        Fade to black-out

EFFECTS PLOT

Author's Note: Scenes of agricultural work — combining, spraying etc. — or of Filipino street scenes may be projected on to the set or backdrop during scene changes, to the accompaniment of sombre music.

ACT I
SCENE 1

Cue 1	At opening *"O Soave Funciulla" from* La Bohème *from CD player*	(Page 1)
Cue 2	**Ivy**: "I shouldn't have said that, sorry." *The CD ends*	(Page 4)
Cue 3	**Martin** presses play on the VCR control *Filipino voices and* **Maria**'s *voice as per text, p. 5*	(Page 4)

Cue 18	**Maria** glances to the doorway *Volvo boot slams, off*	(Page 24)

SCENE 4

Cue 19	At opening *Car doors slam, off*	(Page 26)
Cue 20	**Joe** switches the ghetto blaster on *"Twisting the Night Away" plays*	(Page 27)
Cue 21	**Martin** switches the ghetto blaster off *Music ceases*	(Page 27)
Cue 22	**Martin** bolts the back door *Pickup leaves, off*	(Page 28)
Cue 23	**Martin** switches the CD player on *Music (Verdi); play until end of scene*	(Page 34)

SCENE 5

Cue 24	At scene opening *Poultry sounds from the yard, throughout scene*	(Page 34)
Cue 25	**Maria**: " ... always rustling outside ... " *Hen cackles triumphantly*	(Page 34)
Cue 26	**Maria** inserts a new tape into tape recorder *Voices as per text, p. 35*	(Page 35)
Cue 27	**Maria** switches the tape recorder off *All voices cease*	(Page 35)
Cue 28	**Joe** kisses her face all over *Vehicle stops in the yard, doors open and shut off*	(Page 37)
Cue 29	**Joe** switches his ghetto blaster on *"Baby It's You" plays*	(Page 38)
Cue 30	**Joe** switches ghetto blaster off *Music ceases*	(Page 38)

SCENE 6

Cue 31	At opening *Music (Verdi) plays from CD player; continue until end of scene*	(Page 40)

ACT II
Scene 1